MW00676625

PL/1
Programming Language

Mohammad Dadashzadeh, Ph.D.
Assistant Professor of Decision Sciences
The Wichita State University, Kansas

Research and Education Association
61 Ethel Road West
Piscataway, New Jersey 08854

THE ESSENTIALS OF
PL/1 PROGRAMMING LANGUAGE®

Printed in the United States of America

Library of Congress Catalog Card Number 89-62084

International Standard Book Number 0-87891-695-4

ESSENTIALS is a registered trademark of
Research and Education Association, Piscataway, New Jersey 08854

WHAT "THE ESSENTIALS" WILL DO FOR YOU

This book is a review and study guide. It is comprehensive and it is concise.

It helps in preparing for exams, in doing homework, and remains a handy reference source at all times.

It condenses the vast amount of detail characteristic of the subject matter and summarizes the **essentials** of the field.

It will thus save hours of study and preparation time.

The book provides quick access to the important facts, principles, statements, and programming styles in the field.

Materials needed for exams can be reviewed in summary form – eliminating the need to read and re-read many pages of textbook and class notes. The summaries will even tend to bring detail to mind that had been previously read or noted.

This "ESSENTIALS" book has been prepared by an expert in the field, and has been carefully reviewed to assure accuracy and maximum usefulness.

Dr. Max Fogiel
Program Director

iii

CONTENTS

CHAPTER 1

INTRODUCTION TO PL/1

1.1 BRIEF OVERVIEW OF THE LANGUAGE

Figure 1 shows a PL/1 program which outputs the smallest value, the largest value, and the average value for a series of numbers input to the program. The number of values to be input is itself an input to the program and will be supplied first.

```
PRGRM1: PROCEDURE OPTIONS(MAIN);
        DECLARE COUNT DECIMAL FIXED;

        PUT LIST('How many values will be input?');
        GET LIST(COUNT);

        IF COUNT >= 1 THEN
        BEGIN;
            RUNNING_TOTAL = O;

            PUT SKIP LIST('Enter the first value');
            GET LIST(FIRST_VALUE);
            SMALLEST = FIRST_VALUE; LARGEST = FIRST_VALUE;

            RUNNING_TOTAL = RUNNING_TOTAL + FIRST_VALUE;
```

```
DO I = 2 TO COUNT;
    PUT SKIP LIST('Enter next value');
    GET LIST(VALUE);
    RUNNING_TOTAL = RUNNING_TOTAL + VALUE;

    IF VALUE > LARGEST
        THEN LARGEST = VALUE;
    ELSE IF VALUE < SMALLEST THEN SMALLEST = VALUE;
    END; /* DO */

    PUT SKIP LIST('The smallest value: ', SMALLEST);
    PUT SKIP LIST('The largest value: ', LARGEST);
    PUT SKIP LIST('The average:', RUNNING_TOTAL / COUNT);
    END; /* BEGIN */
END PRGRM1;
```

FIGURE 1

PL/1 is a general-purpose programming language incorpo-
rating many of the features of FORTRAN, ALGOL, and CO-
BOL in addition to other features such as rudimentary string
and list processing. It was originally intended to supplant the
languages it grew out of; although that has not happened, it is
used widely. PL/1 is applicable to a rather wide range of problem areas: scientific applications, business applications, and to
some extent systems programming, as well as applications
which overlap these areas.

It is tempting to describe PL/1 by saying that it has most of
FORTRAN, most of COBOL, a lot of ALGOL, and some of
several special-purpose programming languages. PL/1 contains
fairly direct analogues of the FORTRAN parameter transmission mechanisms, separately compiled subprograms, formatted
input and output, and common blocks; of the ALGOL block
structure and structured programming statements; and of the

2

COBOL record-oriented input-output; heterogenous arrays, and PICTURE type declarations. The language has its roots in these and several other languages, but was designed to balance two sets of conflicting goals: generality and flexibility without loss of execution efficiency, and ease of use for unsophisticated programmers without loss of detailed control for experienced programmers. Generality and flexibility, as well as detailed control by the experienced programmer, are obtained through the inclusion in the language of a large variety of data types, storage classes, data structures, and control mechanisms. Ease of use by the unsophisticated programmer is obtained through extensive default declarations provided by PL/1 compilers whenever the programmer fails to specify all the attributes of a program element. The inexperienced programmer may thus write straightforward programs without concern for many language details, and the compilers are expected to provide the necessary additional information. As additional features are needed, a user can learn PL/1's expanded capabilities.

As Table 1 indicates, PL/1 has most of the operators found in the algebraic languages. It has assignment statements and expressions like FORTRAN, ALGOL, and BASIC. In addition, it has a concatenation operator for joining strings and pointer variables (containing addresses) whereby complex data structures can be manipulated.

An outstanding feature of PL/1 is its richness of data description capabilities. Both arithmetic (binary or decimal) and string (character-string or bit-string) data can be represented. Data may have different attributes (FIXED, FLOAT, and so on). Data may be aggregated into arrays of like elements (similar to FORTRAN and ALGOL) and structures (similar to CO-BOL data structures).

A third dimension of data variability is provided by permitting the user to specify the mode of storage allocation to be

3

DATA TYPES
area, pointer, offset (variables only)
file, picture, label, format, entry (constants or variables)
fixed, float, binary, decimal, real, complex (arithmetic)
bit, char, varying, non-varying (string)

DATA STRUCTURES
scalars
arrays of scalars or structures
structure of scalars, arrays, and other structures

DATA OPERATIONS
+, -, *,/, exponentiation, logical, relational, concatenation (of strings)

CONTROL OPERATIONS
GO TO < label >
IF <expression> THEN <statement> ELSE <statement>
SELECT; WHERE (<logical expression>) <statement>;
...OTHERWISE <statement>; END;
DO <variable> = <expression$_1$> BY <expression$_2$> TO
<expression$_3$>
DO WHILE (<logical expression>)
DO UNTIL (<logical expression>)
CALL, RETURN, STOP, EXIT, LEAVE
ON <condition> <on-unit>
REVERT, SIGNAL

PROGRAM STRUCTURES
groups
DO;

. . .
END;
begin blocks

```
BEGIN;
  . . .
END;
procedure blocks
  <procedure name>:        PROCEDURE (<parameter list>);
                    . . .
  END:
(procedures may be either subroutines or functions)
```

SYSTEM ENVIRONMENT
  generally batch oriented
  library routines
  run-time support of 1/0 and storage allocation

TABLE 1–PL/1 SUMMARY

used for each data representation. If a piece of data is declared STATIC, storage for it is allocated once and for all at program load time (as in FORTRAN) and is not freed until the program terminates. AUTOMATIC storage is allocated upon entry to a block and freed when the block is exited (like ALGOL). Storage is allocated and freed for data declared to be in the CONTROLLED storage class upon specific commands by the program at run time, independent of block boundaries.

Use of variables of the BASED storage class can be quite complex. In fact, a based variable need never have any actual storage allocated to it. In this case, the variable serves as a descriptor of other data. Through BASED and POINTER variables, PL/1 permits simple manipulation of list structures.

There is a good range of control structures, not unlike those found in other languages. There are also some important additions. For example, ON statements permit the user to associate some action (at program execution time) with an event that may occur. For example, the user may write: ON OVERFLOW CALL CHECK_ARGUMENTS;. After this statement has been executed, if overflow interrupts are enabled and an arithmetic overflow occurs in the same block as the ON statement, the routine CHECK_ARGUMENTS will be executed. The occurrence of the condition can be simulated (thereby deliberately causing CHECK_ARGUMENTS to be called) by executing: SIGNAL OVERFLOW;.

The program structures of PL/1 are basically those of ALGOL: block structure, conditional statements, and loops. A subroutine may be invoked as a separate task. One feature not usually found in high-level languages is the ability to have compile-time macros. These permit, among other things, the calculation of indices or constants at compile time to permit greater execution efficiency without writing an excessive number of statements.

A distinguishing feature of most PL/1 implementations is their size. The complexity of the language makes a compiler and support packages for the full language quite large. Because the language was initially designed in the early 1960s before conversational processing was well developed, its features are not particularly suited to interactive usage. However, some derivatives of the language have been specially designed for interactive use. Because of its size and heritage (it originated with IBM and some of its major users), the language has been available primarily on IBM mainframes, although PL/1 compilers for Burroughs (UNISYS), Control Data, and Digital Equipment compilers have been developed. Subset PL/1 compilers have also been developed for educational use by Cornell University and for microcomputer development by Microsoft Corporation.

1.2 LANGUAGE COMPONENTS

1.2.1 CHARACTER SET

There are 60 characters in the PL/1 language. They include the extended alphabet of 29 characters: A-Z, @, #, and $; 10 decimal digits; 21 special characters including " " blank, "=" equal or assignment symbol, "+" plus sign, "−" minus sign, "*" asterisk or multiplication symbol, "/ " slash or divide symbol, "(" left parenthesis, ")" right parenthesis, "," comma, "." point or period, " ' " single quotation mark or apostrophe, "%" percent symbol, ";" semicolon, ":" colon, " ^ " NOT symbol, "&" AND symbol, "|" OR symbol, ">" greater than symbol, "<" less than symbol, "_" underscore, and "?" question mark.

Special characters may be combined to create other symbols. For example, "<=" means less than or equal to, and "**" denotes exponentiation. Blanks are not permitted in such character combinations.

1.2.2 IDENTIFIERS

Identifiers are names of variables (COUNT, RUNNING_TOTAL, FIRST_VALUE, SMALLEST, LARGEST, VALUE in program PRGRM1 of Figure 1), names of procedures (PRGRM1 in the same program), names of files (there are no explicitly defined files in PRGRM1), labels of PL/1 statements (only the PROCEDURE statement in PRGRM1 is labeled), and *Keywords* (such as PUT or GET).

An identifier for variables, labels, and *internal* procedures may be from 1 to 31 alphabetic characters (A-Z, @, #, and $), numeric digits (0-9), and the underscore character (_). However, the first character of an identifier must be alphabetic, and there may be no blanks within the identifier. The underscore character should be used in identifiers to improve readability

7

(NET_INCOME as opposed to NETINCOME). There are *no* reserved words in PL/1.

A procedure with an OPTIONS(MAIN) is called an *external* procedure. Identifiers of external procedures and files are a maximum of seven or eight characters, depending on the operating system environment which you are using.

1.2.3   STATEMENTS

PL/1 is said to be free-form, that is, a statement may contain blanks as needed to improve readability and it may span several lines. The end of a PL/1 statement is signified by a semicolon. As such, one line may contain several PL/1 statements each of which is terminated by a semicolon.

Because PL/1 is free-form, no special coding sheets are required. However, the first position (column) on a line cannot be used. In general, it is desirable to have no more than one statement per line. In many cases, it is appropriate to break a statement into smaller parts and code them on separate lines using indentation to highlight logical grouping of program code.

1.2.4   CONSTANTS

A *constant* is a data item that does not have a name (an identifier) and whose value cannot change during the execution of the program. There are six types of PL/1 constants.

1) **Decimal Fixed-Point Constants** are used in almost all programs. They consist of one or more decimal digits and, optionally, a decimal point. Some examples are: −123, 12.75, +9.09, 0.007, and 32767.

2) **Decimal Floating-Point Constants** are written using scientific notation. For example, the value 123 in decimal float-

ing-point could be written as: 1.23E+01, where E+01 indicates a multiplier with the value 10^{+01}. Therefore, E+01 *floats* the decimal point to the right 01 places so that the value is 123. Other examples of decimal floating-point numbers are: -12.09E1 (-120.9), and 1.33E-03 (0.00133).

3) **Character String Constants** are data items that may include any of the up to 256 characters recognized by the computer system. Blanks included in a character string are considered part of it and are included in the count of the length of the string. Character string constants must be enclosed in single quotation marks. If an apostrophe is needed within the character string constant, it must be written as two single quotation marks with no intervening blanks. Examples are: 'THE SMALLEST VALUE IS: ', and '10% OF EMPLOYEE''S GROSS PAY IS – = >'.

It is also possible to specify a *repetition factor* for character string constants. For example, (5) '– =' is an equivalent way of specifying character string constant '– = – = – = – = – ='.

4) **Bit-String Constants** are written as a series of binary digits (i.e., 0s and 1s) enclosed in single quotation marks and followed by the letter B. Examples are: '1'B, '10110'B, and (7)'1'B, where in the latter (7) is a repetition factor. Bit strings are typically used to indicate whether or not a certain condition exists, that is, they are normally used to indicate true or false.

5) **Binary Fixed-Point** constants such as 101B are rarely used.

6) **Binary Floating-Point Constants** such as 0.1101101E+32B are used in highly specialized scientific applications.

1.3   AN ANNOTATED EXAMPLE

This section provides an annotated example of some of the intermediate features of PL/1. It is intended primarily to familiarize readers with reading PL/1 programs even though some of the concepts will be unfamiliar to inexperienced programmers. Figure 2 depicts a PL/1 program consisting of a main program called PRGRM2 and a subprogram entitled SUM. The subprogram SUM is a function which sums the elements of its single argument, an array of real numbers formally called V. The main program creates a sequence of arrays from values in the standard input file. The values in each array are specified in the input file following the number representing the size (i.e., number of values) of the array. The following annotations refer to

```
1   PRGRM2: PROCEDURE OPTIONS(MAIN);
2   ON ENDFILE(SYSIN) STOP;
3   START: GET LIST(N);
4         IF N > O THEN BEGIN;
5                   DECLARE A(N) DECIMAL FLOAT;
6                   GET LIST(A);
7                   PUT SKIP LIST( 'INPUT IS', A,
8                                   'SUM IS', SUM(A) );
9                   GO TO START;
10                  END; /* BEGIN */
11  SUM: PROCEDURE(V);
12  DECLARE V(*) DECIMAL FLOAT;
13  DECLARE TEMP DECIMAL FLOAT INITIAL(O);
14  DO I = 1 TO DIM(V,1);
15  TEMP = TEMP + V(I);
16  END; /* DO */
17  RETURN(TEMP);
18  END SUM;
19  END PRGRM2;
```

FIGURE 2

10

the line numbers in Figure 2, which are not part of the actual program.

Line 1. Beginning of the main program. The main program takes the form of a PROCEDURE declaration. It is named PRGRM2. The OPTIONS(MAIN) attribute specifies that this procedure is the main program.

Line 2. First executable statement in the main program. This ON ENDFILE statement tells the system input routine what to do *when* the end-of-file is encountered. In this case, the programmer-specified action is to STOP the program.

Line 3. The statement is labeled START. Integer variable N is declared implicitly by use. A value for the variable N is to be read in from the standard input file. The GET indicates input; the LIST indicates that the input value will appear on the standard input file as a decimal value separated from other data items by blanks or commas.

Line 4. An IF-THEN statement begins here and extends to line 10. If the test $N > O$ is not satisfied, then control transfers to the first executable statement following line 10, which in this case is line 19, the terminating END for the main program.

Line 5. Lines 5-10 form a BEGIN block which is executed if the test on line 4 is satisfied. The block begins with a declaration of an array of N elements, where the value of N is the value just read in. The DECIMAL FLOAT specification gives the data type of each element in the array A. The BEGIN block, in addition to grouping statements, also governs storage allocation. When such a block is set up, storage for any variables declared within its boundaries will be allocated dynamically each time it is executed rather than once and for all at the start of the program. Then, once the sequence of events takes the program out of the block's boundaries, that storage is relinquished. Should the block be entered again, storage will be allocated anew. Therefore, a new array A is created *each time* control enters this block during program execution, and the array is *destroyed* on block exit.

Line 6. N values for the newly created array A are read in from the standard input file. Again, LIST-directed input is used so that the values may be entered in the file separated by blanks or commas without any special formatting.

Lines 7–8. These two lines contain one PL/1 statement. PUT indicates output to the standard output file. LIST-directed output is used which requires no format specifications by the programmer. Output values are printed beginning at *predetermined tab positions*. The input values in A are printed, together with the sum of the values returned by the function SUM, with appropriate headings.

Line 9. Control is transferred back to line 3 to begin another loop.

Line 10. End of the BEGIN block begun on line 4, as well as the end of the IF-THEN statement started on the same line. A comment (enclosed within /* and */) signifies this END to be associated with a matching BEGIN.

Lines 11–18. Definition of the function subprogram SUM. This definition (declaration) could have been placed anywhere within the body of the main program. The PL/1 compilers are expected to process all declarations appearing anywhere within a program as though they had occurred at the beginning of the program.

Line 11. Beginning of the procedure named SUM, which has one formal parameter, V.

Line 12. PL/1 requires declarations of all formal parameters. V is declared to be an array of decimal floating-point numbers. The * in the subscript list for V designates that the subscript range is to be that of the actual parameter array transmitted to SUM.

Line 13. A local variable TEMP is declared to be of decimal floating-point type and to have an initial value of zero. A new variable TEMP, initialized to zero, is created on each entry to SUM and destroyed on exit.

Line 14. A DO iteration begins here and ends with the END on line 16. The function call DIM(V,1) invokes a built-in PL/1 function which returns the size (subscript range) of the first dimension of array V; thus it is possible to find out the size of an array dynamically during execution. The loop variable I is initialized to 1 and incremented by 1 each time through the loop until the size of array V is reached. The undeclared loop variable I is assumed by PL/1 compiler to be a global fixed-point variable.

Line 15. Body of the iteration statement begun on line 14. The successive elements of the array V are summed using the temporary variable TEMP.

Line 16. End of the DO statement begun on line 14.

Line 17. Control is transferred back to the calling program. Since SUM is a function subprogram, and expression designating the function value to be returned must be given, which in this case simply consists of the value of variable TEMP.

Line 18. End of the body of subprogram SUM.

Line 19. End of the main program.

CHAPTER 2

DATA TYPES AND OPERATIONS

2.1 THE *DECLARE* STATEMENT

The statement used to *explicitly* define the data type of a variable is the DECLARE statement. Variables not declared in a DECLARE statement will be given a *default declaration* by PL/1 compiler. Specifically, identifiers beginning with the letters I through N will be assumed to designate whole numbers, whereas identifiers beginning with the letters A through H, O through Z, and the symbols @, #, and $ will be assumed to be in the floating-point format.

DECLARE statements may appear anywhere following the PROCEDURE statement. Although it is common to find DECLARE statements grouped together at the beginning of a PL/1 program, it is *not* necessary for a DECLARE statement to precede the declared variable's use in a PL/1 statement.

A DECLARE statement begins with the keyword DECLARE and contains one or more variable identifiers along with the type of data to be stored in each variable. The words used to describe the type of data are called *attributes.* For example, the statement, DECLARE PRICE DECIMAL FIXED(5,2) INITIAL(321.45);, declares the variable identified by PRICE to have the *base attribute* DECIMAL, the *scale attribute* FIXED, the *precision attribute* (5,2), and the *initial attribute* or value of 321.45.

The base attribute can be either DECIMAL or BINARY. The scale attribute can be either FIXED or FLOAT. The precision attribute specifies the number of significant digits and/or the decimal or binary point alignment. Specifically, DECLARE NUMBER DECIMAL FIXED(7,2); specifies that NUMBER may contain up to seven decimal digits of which two are fractional. If there are no fractional digits, then the comma and the second digit of the precision attribute are omitted: DECLARE NUMBER DECIMAL FIXED(7);. Another way in which the preceding statement could be written is: DECLARE NUMBER FIXED DECIMAL(7);, where the keywords DECIMAL and FIXED are reversed. Most attributes can appear in any order as long as the precision attribute follows either the base or the scale attribute.

For floating-point data, do not specify fractions in the precision attribute and declare only the number of significant digits. For example: DECLARE NUMBER FLOAT DECIMAL(12);.

PL/1 supports COMPLEX data (values consisting of two parts: a real part and a signed imaginary part) through standard arithmetic operations and a *mode attribute* in the DECLARE statement. For example, DECLARE (ROOT1, ROOT2) FLOAT DECIMAL(6) COMPLEX; specifies the variables ROOT1 and ROOT2 to be complex variables with real and imaginary parts that are declared to be floating-point decimal with six significant digits. Notice that one DECLARE statement can be used to declare two or more variables which have the same data type by enclosing the variable identifiers (names) in parentheses and separating them with a comma.

When declaring *string* data, which are a sequence of characters or bits, the precision attribute is referred to as the *length attribute*. For example, to declare variable PART_DESCRIPTION to be of type CHARACTER (abbreviated by CHAR), a maximum length must be decided upon: DECLARE PART_DESCRIPTION CHAR(20). After this declaration, assigning a character string constant longer than 20 characters to PART_DESCRIPTION will result in the extra characters to the right to be truncated. Assigning a character string constant shorter than 20 characters will result in padding on the right with blank characters. If this padding on the right is not desired, then the character variable must be declared with the *varying attribute*: DECLARE PART_DESCRIPTION CHAR(20) VARYING;.

String data also encompasses variables declared to be of type BIT. In particular, to establish flags and indicators related to the programming of I/O operations, declare them to be of type BIT with a length of 1. For example, the following code segment provides a template for processing an undetermined number of input values.

```
DECLARE MORE-VALUES BIT(1);
DECLARE NO            BIT(1) INITIAL('0'B);
DECLARE YES           BIT(1) INITIAL('1'B);
. . .
/* MORE_VALUES WILL BE SET TO NO IF NO MORE INPUT IS
            AVAILABLE. */
ON ENDFILE(SYSIN) MORE_VALUES = NO;

MORE_VALUES = YES;
/*INITIALIZE MORE_VALUES TO YES.*/
```

```
/* AS LONG AS THERE ARE MORE VALUES TO PROCESS. */
DO WHILE(MORE_VALUES = YES)

      . . .

END;
```

Finally, as already indicated, a declared variable can be assigned a value by the initial attribute. An example to initialize a character variable is: DECLARE REPORT_HEADING CHAR(20) INITIAL('RESEARCH AND EDUCATION ASSOCIATION');. Of course, variables could be initialized by an assignment statement in the program (e.g., DECLARE REPORT_HEADING CHAR(20); REPORT_HEADING = 'RESEARCH AND EDUCATION ASSOCIATION';). The simple rule to use is that those variables that will remain constant during the execution of a program (e.g., REPORT_ HEADING or YES in the above code segment) should be given an INITIAL attribute, whereas those variables that must be initialized but will assume different values in the course of execution of the program are best not given an INITIAL attribute, and rather, should be initialized by assignment statements at the beginning of the program.

2.2   ARITHMETIC OPERATIONS AND BUILT-IN FUNCTIONS

The PL/1 symbols for the five basic arithmetic operations are: +, −, *, /, and ** (exponentiation). These operators are used along with variables and constants to form *arithmetic expressions* which can be used anywhere a constant value could be used. Examples are: $(A + B)$ and $2*A + B**.5$. There are three rules that PL/1 follows in evaluating an arithmetic expression. First, the *order of precedence* for arithmetic operators is: 1) negation (as in −A) and exponentiation; 2) multiplication and division; and 3) addition and subtraction. Second, if two or more operators of the same precedence appear in the same expression, the order of evaluation of those operators is from *right to left*. Third, when parentheses are specified, the expression within the parentheses will be evaluated first, starting with the innermost pair of parentheses.

For example, in the arithmetic expression A + B * C, the order of evaluation is multiplication then addition. In evaluating A ** B ** C, B is first raised to the power of C, then A is raised to the resulting value. On the other hand, (A ** B) ** C is evaluated by first raising A to the power of B and then raising the result to the power of C. Finally, A ** (−B * C) is evaluated by first negating B, next multiplying it by C, and then raising A to the resulting power.

Built-in functions are PL/1 supplied procedures that produce (return) a new value for each value or set of values they receive. For example, SQRT is a function that accepts a single input value and returns the square root of that input value. Functions can be referenced anywhere a constant could be used, e.g., PUT SKIP LIST('THE SQUARE ROOT OF ', X, ' IS: ', SQRT(X));. The number of input values expected by functions varies. SQRT is an example of a function with one argument (i.e., input value). The MOD function expects two arguments and returns the remainder resulting from the division of the first argument by the second argument, e.g., MOD(34,5) returns the value 4. Table 2 illustrates some of the built-in arithmetic functions provided by PL/1.

2.3 MIXING DATA TYPES

In general, arithmetic operations on mixed data types should be avoided. When mixed data types appear in an arithmetic expression, PL/1 compiler automatically inserts appropriate instructions to convert data types to another format. The rules for these conversions are: 1) if the *base* of the data items

Built-in function	Purpose	Example
ABS	Finds the absolute value of its argument.	A = ABS(–3.14); /* A = 3.14 */
CEIL	Finds smallest integer not exceeding its argument.	A = CEIL(–3.14); /* A = –3.00 */
FLOOR	Finds largest integer not exceeding its argument.	A = FLOOR(–3.14); /* A = –4.00 */
LOG10	Finds logarithm of its argument to base 10.	A = LOG10(1000); /* A = 3.00 */
MIN	Finds smallest value from its two or more arguments.	A = MIN(–3, 2.00, –4); /* A = –4.00 */
SIGN	Finds the sign of its argument. (Returns –1, 0, or +1.)	I = SIGN(123.45); /* 1 = 1 */
SIND	Finds the sine of its argument (assumed to be in degrees).	A = SIND(90); /* A = 1.00 */
TRUNC	Finds the integer part of its argument.	A = TRUNC(12.9); /* A = 12.00 */

Table 2–Some PL/1 arithmetic built-in functions.

differ, DECIMAL is converted to BINARY; and 2) if the *scale* of the data items differ, FIXED is converted to FLOAT. For example, consider the following code segment:

```
DECLARE A FIXED DECIMAL;
DECLARE B FLOAT DECIMAL;
```

```
A = 123;
B = 32;
M = (A + B) /2;
```

During execution, the decimal value 32 is converted to floating-point representation (3.2E+01) and stored in variable B. Next, in evaluating (A + B)/2, because the scales of variables A and B are different, the value of A is first converted to FLOATING DECIMAL, i.e., 12.3E+01, before the sum, 15.5E+01, is determined. Also, the constant 2 is converted to FLOATING DECIMAL 0.2E+01. Finally, since M has not been explicitly declared, it is assumed to be BINARY FIXED(15,0), and thus, it will be assigned only the integer portion of the quotient of the division of 15.5E+01 by 0.2E+01, i.e., 77. Table 3 lists the default attributes for partially declared variables.

2.4   STRING-HANDLING FUNCTIONS

PL/1 supports a single operation for string data. The operation is called *concatenation* and is denoted by two vertical bars, I I. The concatenation operator joins together string (character or bit) data. For example, the following code segment is permissible in PL/1:

```
FIRST_NAME = 'ESMAEEL';
MIDDLE_NAME= 'REZA';
LAST_NAME ='DADASHZADEH';
BLANK = ' '; COMMA = ',';
FULL_NAME = LAST_NAME I I COMMA I I BLANK I I
              FIRST_NAME I I BLANK I I MIDDLE_NAME;
/* FULL_NAME IS NOW "DADASHZADEH, ESMAEEL REZA" */
```

PL/1 provides a number of string-handling functions. The SUBSTR function produces a *substring* of a given string by

20

Declared Attributes	Default Attributes
DECIMAL FIXED	(5,0)
DECIMAL FLOAT	(6)
BINARY FIXED	(15,0)
BINARY FLOAT	(21)
DECIMAL	FLOAT(6)
BINARY	FLOAT(21)
FIXED	DECIMAL(5,0)
FLOAT	DECIMAL(6)
none (initial character I–N)	BINARY FIXED(15)
none (initial character not I–N)	DECIMAL FLOAT(6)

Table 3–Default attributes for partially declared identifiers.

taking three arguments, a string, the starting position within the character string from which a substring will be extracted, and number of characters to be extracted. For example, SUBSTR(LAST_NAME, 7, 5) will return 'ZADEH'.

The SUBSTR function in PL/1 may also play the role of a *pseudo-variable* by appearing on the left hand side of an assignment statement. Specifically, SUBSTR(FULL_NAME, 12, 2) = '**'; replaces the two characters starting at position 12 of the current value for FULL_NAME with two asterisks.

The function CHAR when used with a single argument returns the character string representation of its numeric input. For example, the assignment statements I = 123; and A = CHAR(I); result in character variable A assuming the string value '123'. When used with two arguments, the CHAR function returns a character string of the length specified by its second argument and which consists of the character string representation of its numeric first argument. For example, I = 123;

and $A = CHAR(I, 5)$ result in character variable A being assigned the value ' 123'.

Table 4 illustrates some of the string-handling functions, as well as the useful DATE and TIME functions built in PL/1.

Built-in function	Purpose/Example
DATE	Returns the current date in the form YYMMDD. DATE should be declared to have the BUILTIN attribute. DECLARE DATE BUILTIN; DECLARE TODAY CHAR(6); TODAY = DATE;
TIME	Returns the time of day in the form HHMMSSTTT, where TTT = milliseconds. DECLARE TIME BUILTIN; DECLARE START_TIME CHAR(9); START_TIME = TIME;
INDEX	Takes two arguments. The first is the source string to be searched for the substring specified by the second argument. If the substring is found, the starting position for its leftmost character within the source string is returned. Otherwise, INDEX returns zero. DECLARE SENTENCE CHAR(40) VARYING; SENTENCE = 'TRUTH HURTS!'; I = INDEX(SENTENCE, 'UR'); /* I = 8 */
LENGTH	Finds the length of a given bit or character string. DECLARE NAME CHAR(20) VARYING; NAME = 'DOE, JOHN'; L = LENGTH(NAME); /* L = 9 */

22

REPEAT   Concatenates the string given as its first argument
                  with itself n times, where n is the second argu-
                  ment.
                  DECLARE TITLE_LINE CHAR(10);
                  TITLE_LINE = REPEAT('– =', 5);
                  /* TITLE–LINE = '– = – = – = – = – =' */

TRANSLATE   Takes three arguments. The first argument is a
                  source string, some of whose characters are to be
                  translated. The third argument indicates those
                  characters to be translated. The middle argument,
                  which must be of the same length as the third,
                  provides the replacement characters in a one-to-
                  one mapping.
                  DECLARE EDIT_TODAY CHAR(8);
                  EDIT_TODAY = TRANSLATE('MO/DA/YR', DATE,
                  'YRMODA');

Table4 PL/1 string-handling and built-in DATE and TIME functions.

CHAPTER 3

LOGICAL TESTING

3.1 THE *IF* STATEMENT

When a statement or sequence of statements, S, is to be executed only when a certain condition specified by the logical expression, *E,* is true (i.e., has the value '1'B), the IF statement is used. The IF statement takes one of the following forms:

(i) IF *E* THEN *S*

(ii) IF *E* THEN *S1* ELSE *S2*

Here, *E* denotes a *logical expression,* and S, *S1,* and *S2* designate any executable statement, *DO group,* or *BEGIN block.* Note that no semicolon explicitly appears to terminate the IF statement. However, S, *S1,* and *S2* each terminates with a semicolon, so that the semicolon will appear in any event.

Execution of the first form of the IF statement occurs in two steps. First, the logical expression *E* is evaluated, giving a true or false result. If the result is true, then *S* is executed; otherwise, *S* is bypassed. Execution of the second form of the IF statement is similar, except that either *S1* or *S2* is executed

24

and the other is bypassed, depending on whether the result of evaluating E is true or false, respectively.

In PL/1, a *logical expression* is either a 1-bit string constant ('0'B or '1'B), a 1-bit variable, a function reference which returns a 1-bit string constant as a result, a comparison between two arithmetic expressions or two string expressions, or a series of such logical expressions connected by the logical operators & (and), | (or), and ^ (not). A comparison is formed by separating two expressions by one of the comparison operators <, <=, =, ^=, >=, or >. When applied to arithmetic expressions, the comparison operators reflect the usual ordering that exists between numbers. When applied to string expressions, the comparison operators reflect the so-called *collating sequence* or predefined ordering that exists among the characters in the character set. The comparison operators share the same precedence with each other, but have higher precedence than the logical operators, and lower precedence than the arithmetic operators. Moreover, in evaluating a logical expression & has precedence over |, and ^ has precedence over both & and |. Parentheses can be used to override this precedence, just as for arithmetic expressions.

The IF statement is designed to execute *one* statement following the THEN or ELSE. However, a *DO group* or a *BEGIN block* can be used to execute more than one statement following the THEN or ELSE. The DO group (or BEGIN block) is simply a series of PL/1 statements headed by the keyword "DO;" (or "BEGIN;") and terminated by the keyword "END;".

The following program segment computes the number of real roots, NUMBER_OF_ROOTS, and their values, $X1$ and $X2$, given coefficients A, B, and C of the quadratic equation: $Ax^2 + Bx + C = 0$.

```
DETERMINANT = B**2 - 4*A*C;
IF DETERMINANT < O
    THEN NUMBER_OF_ROOTS = O;
    ELSE IF DETERMINANT = O
        THEN DO;
            NUMBER_OF_ROOTS = 1;
            X1, X2 = -B / (2*A);
        END;
        ELSE DO;
            NUMBER_OF_ROOTS = 2;
            X1 = (-B + D**.5) / (2*A);
            X2 = (-B - SQRT(D)) / (2*A);
        END;
```

The nested IF statements, IF *E1* THEN IF *E2* THEN *S1*; ELSE *S2;*, raise the question of which IF the ELSE refers to. In PL/1, the ELSE is always associated with the last preceding IF for which an ELSE is not already specified. In this example, *S2* *is* executed if both *E1* and *E2* are true. If we intend *S2* to be executed when *E1* *is* false, then a *null ELSE* statement (i.e., an ELSE followed immediately with a semicolon) could be used as follows: IF *E1* THEN IF *E2* THEN *S1*; **ELSE**; ELSE *S2;*.

3.2   THE *SELECT* STATEMENT

The SELECT statement allows selection of *one* from a series of alternative statements, depending on the value of a logical expression. It has the following form:

```
SELECT;
    WHEN (E1)    S1
    WHEN (E2)    S2
       . . .
    OTHERWISE   Sn
END;
```

Here, the *E*'s designate logical expressions, and the *S*'s denote the corresponding statements to be executed when the associated *E* is true. *Sn* is the statement to be executed if none of the *E*'s evaluate to true. Note that the order of the logical expressions and their corresponding statements in the SELECT statement is significant since only the *first* logical expression to yield '1'B (i.e., evaluates to true) will cause its associated statement to be executed.

The SELECT statement provides a convenient way of abbreviating a series of nested IF statements. Witness the following reformulation of the program segment of the last section:

```
DETERMINANT = B ** 2 - 4 * A * C;
SELECT;
WHEN (DETERMINANT < 0) NUMBER_OF_ROOTS = 0;
WHEN (DETERMINANT = 0 ) DO; NUMBER_OF_ROOTS = 1;
                 X1, X2 = -B / (2 * A); END;
OTHERWISE   DO;
                 NUMBER_OF_ROOTS = 2;
                 X1 = (-B +D ** .5) / (2 * A);
                 X2 = (-B - D ** .5) / (2 * A);
             END;
END;
```

3.3   CONDITIONS AND *ON*-UNITS

During the execution of a program a variety of special conditions can arise. Some conditions such as overflow or underflow, and division by zero are monitored by hardware. Other conditions such as reading past end of file, subscript out of range, and end of page are monitored by software. These problems will interrupt the normal processing of the program and transfer control from the program to the operating system which attempts a default action *unless* the programmer tells it

27

otherwise by means of an ON statement.

The ON statement is designed to allow the programmer to specify the action that should be taken when an interrupt occurs from an *enabled* condition. In PL/1, *condition prefixes* are used to enable or disable interrupts. A condition prefix takes the form, (condition): statement, where statement is a labeled or unlabeled executable statement. The appearance of a condition prefix such as, (SUBSCRIPTRANGE): A(I) = I;, denotes that the named condition is enabled for the remainder of the *block* in which the statement appears. Just as a disabled condition can be enabled with a prefix, so can an enabled condition be disabled by adding the "NO" prefix to the condition name, e.g., (NOSUBSCRIPTRANGE): A(J) = J;.

The ON statement has the general form: ON condition action;, where condition denotes the name of a condition and action is either a single PL/1 statement (no DO groups or DO loops) or it is a BEGIN block. For example, ON ENDFILE(SYSIN) NO_MORE_DATA = 'YES';. The ON statement is an executable statement and upon execution *establishes* the action to be taken. *The action is taken only if and when the condition arises later in the program.*

There are two ways to cancel the action or on-unit established by an ON statement. First, using the word SYSTEM as the action to be taken in an ON statement will restore the standard default action as the action to be taken when the condition is subsequently raised. Second, the statement REVERT condition; will cause the cancelation of the last ON statement in the same block it appears in.

Finally, the programmer may define her own condition and subsequently raise the condition using the SIGNAL statement. This is a powerful debugging tool that is explored further in Chapter 11 .

CHAPTER 4

LOOPING

4.1   THE *DO WHILE* STATEMENT

The most important way in which the sequence of statements executed differs from the sequence that appears in the program text is that the execution of certain groups of statements will be repeated. In PL/1, the scope of repetition, that is, what portion of the program is to be repeated, is delimited by the keywords DO and END. But PL/1 offers a variety of ways of specifying how many times the execution is to be repeated.

The general format of the DO WHILE statement is:

```
DO WHILE (E);
    S1;
    S2;
    . . .
    Sn;
END;
```

Here, the PL/1 statements *S1, S2, ...,* and *Sn* are collectively referred to as the *body of the loop*, and the statement is executed as follows:

1. The logical expression *E* is evaluated. If the result is '0'B (i.e., false) then execution of the loop is completed. Otherwise, proceed to step 2.

2. The body of the loop is executed. When the last statement of the body (i.e., *Sn)* has been executed, return to step 1.

Note that the test of the WHILE condition, i.e., determining if the logical expression *E* evaluates to false, is made before the loop is executed; hence, the loop may be executed *zero* times (if the initial value of *E* is false). Also note that if the value of *E* is initially '1'B (i.e., true), then some statement in the body of the loop should affect the value of *E*. If not, the loop will continue forever. Finally, note that the value of *E* is not continuously monitored during the execution of the body of the loop. If execution of a statement in the body makes *E* to evaluate to false, that fact is not discovered until after the complete body of the loop has been executed and *E* is being reevaluated prior to the next potential repetition.

One final note is that the parentheses enclosing the logical expression *E* are required while there is no such requirement for logical expressions appearing in the IF or SELECT statements.

The following program segment reads and adds an indeterminate number of input values whose end is signified by the sentinel value −1.

```
SUM = 0;
GET LIST( VALUE );
DO WHILE (VALUE ^ = −1 );
    SUM = SUM + VALUE;
    GET LIST( VALUE );
END;
```

4.2 THE *DO UNTIL* STATEMENT

The DO UNTIL PL/1 statement, which may or may not be available in the compiler you are using, has the general form:

```
DO UNTIL (E);
    S1;
    S2;
    . . .
    Sn;
END;
```

It differs from the DO WHILE in two important ways. First, the logical expression E is evaluated after execution of the body of the loop. Thus, the body of the loop will always be executed at least once. Second, the effect of the logical expression is reversed; the DO UNTIL is terminated when E evaluates to true (DO WHILE terminates when E is false).

The previous example can be rewritten as follows:

```
SUM = 0;
DO UNTIL (VALUE = –1);
    GET LIST( VALUE );
    IF VALUE ^ = –1 THEN SUM = SUM + VALUE;
END;
```

4.3 THE *DO* STATEMENT

The *DO loop* construct allows us to specify a *control (or index) variable* whose value is automatically changed for each repetition of the body of the loop. The PL/1 iterative DO statement takes one of the following forms:

(i)   DO i = m1 TO m2 BY m3;

(ii) DO i = m*1* TO m*2*;

(iii) DO i = m*1* BY m*3*;

(iv) DO i = v*1*, v*2*, ..., v*n*;

Here, i denotes a variable; and m*1*, m*2*, m*3*, v*1*, v*2*, ..., v*n* designate arithmetic expressions. In each of these forms, the DO statement is used to control the repeated execution of some sequence of statements, i.e., the body of the loop, that follow the DO statement and are terminated by an END statement.

In form (i), m*1* represents the initial value for the control variable i, m*2* the final value that the control variable can assume before the loop is terminated, and m*3* the magnitude of the change in the control variable for each repetition. In general, m*3* can be negative as well as positive. Also, the loop variable i need not be an integer value. With a noninteger control variable, a noninteger increment or decrement can be specified.

Several important properties of the DO statement should be kept in mind. First, the values of the arithmetic expressions m*1*, m*2*, and m*3* are determined before the execution of the loop. Nothing that happens in the body of the loop can affect these control values. Second, the test to determine if the control variable has surpassed the final value is performed before any of the statements in the body of the loop are executed; thus, it is possible for the body of the loop not to be executed at all. Third, it is not necessary to use the control variable in the body of the loop. Fourth, the value of the control variable can be changed by statements in the body of the loop, but doing so affects the control of repetition and is a risky practice that should be avoided. Finally, the control variable is incremented (or decremented) and tested after the last execution of the body of the loop and its final value is not the same as its value during the last execution of the body of the loop.

Form (ii) is an abbreviation of form (i) when the increment value is 1. Form (iii) is used when termination of the loop is not naturally specifiable by an upper limit; thus, no test for exit will be automatically performed and the programmer must ensure that some other means (either a GO TO or a LEAVE statement) are provided by which the loop will eventually terminate. Form (iv) is used when the succession of values taken on by the control variable is not a sequence having a constant increment or decrement. In this form of the DO statement, the control variable may be a character string.

Finally, it is also possible to include a WHILE option or an UNTIL option in each of the four forms of the DO statement.

The following two program segments illustrate the PL/1 iterative DO statement.

```
/*Given positive integer X, compute X! = X (X – 1) (X – 2)...(2) (1)*/
/* Note the optional use of labels ABORT and LOOP */
DECLARE X BINARY FIXED;
GET LIST(X);
IF X < 1 THEN ABORT: DO; PUT SKIP LIST('UNDEFINED!');
                 STOP; END ABORT;
ELSE DO;
        F = X;
        LOOP: DO I = X–1 TO 2 BY –1;
            F = F * I;
        END LOOP;
        PUT SKIP LIST('FACTORIAL(', X,') = ', F);
END;
```

```
/* Generate a list of prime numbers less than 100 */
PUT SKIP LIST(2);
/* Print the first (and only even) prime number in the list */
OUTER_LOOP: DO N = 3 TO 100 BY 2;
    FLAG = '1'B; /* Assume N is prime */
    INNER_LOOP: DO M = 3 TO FLOOR(SQRT(N)) BY 2;
        IF MOD(N, M) = 0
        THEN DO;
            FLAG = '0'B; /* Has a divisor; Not prime */
            LEAVE; /* Exit inner loop */
        END;
    END INNER LOOP;
    IF FLAG THEN PUT SKIP LIST(N);
END OUTER_LOOP;
```

4.4   THE *GO TO* STATEMENT

The statements in a PL/1 program are generally executed in the order in which they are written unless a statement is encountered which can alter that order. One such statement is the GO TO statement which has the following general form: GO TO label;.

Here, "label" denotes the label of some other statement between the program's first PROCEDURE statement and its END statement (including the END statement itself). Any PL/1 executable statement can thus be the target of a GO TO statement with the exception of the PROCEDURE statement, the DECLARE statement, the FORMAT statement, and the ON statement. A statement is labeled by prefixing it with a "label" and a colon (:).

In fact, the GO TO statement can have either a *label constant* or a *label variable* as its argument. For example, if L has been declared to be a label and has the value

INNER_LOOP, then GO TO L; would be equivalent to GO TO INNER_LOOP;. However, the use of label variables make the program difficult to understand. The only exception is the use of an array of labels as demonstrated by the following program segment:

```
DECLARE L(1:4) LABEL;
IF (J < 1) | (J > 4) THEN GO TO L_OTHERWISE;
GO TO L(J);
L(1): PUT SKIP LIST('J IS ONE');
GO TO L_END;
L(2): PUT SKIP LIST('J IS TWO');
GO TO L_END;
L(3): PUT SKIP LIST('J IS THREE');
GO TO L_END;
L(4): PUT SKIP LIST('J IS FOUR');
GO TO L_END;
L_OTHERWISE: PUT SKIP LIST('J < 1 OR J > 4');
L_END:
```

Here, L is declared as an array of four elements each of which can contain the label of some statement. The statement GO TO L(J); would branch to one of L(1), L(2), L(3), or L(4) label prefixes, depending on the value of J. The same effect may be achieved by the less efficient SELECT construction below:

```
SELECT;
    WHEN (J = 1) PUT SKIP LIST('J IS ONE');
    WHEN (J = 2) PUT SKIP LIST('J IS TWO');
    WHEN (J = 3) PUT SKIP LIST('J IS THREE');
    WHEN (J = 4) PUT SKIP LIST('J IS FOUR');
    OTHERWISE PUT SKIP LIST('J < 1 OR J > 4');
END;
```

or equivalently by:

```
SELECT (J);
    WHEN (1) PUT SKIP LIST('J IS ONE');
    WHEN (2) PUT SKIP LIST('J IS TWO');
    WHEN (3) PUT SKIP LIST('J IS THREE');
    WHEN (4) PUT SKIP LIST('J IS FOUR');
    OTHERWISE PUT SKIP LIST('J < 1 OR J > 4');
END;
```

CHAPTER 5

DATA STRUCTURES

5.1 ARRAYS

An array is a table of data items in which each item has the same characteristics as every other item in the array. In PL/1, storage for an array is reserved by means of a DECLARE statement which specifies lower and upper *bounds* of the array. For example, DECLARE INCOME(1981:1991) FIXED DECIMAL (6);, specifies an array with 11 elements. In this case, the lower bound is 1981 and the upper bound is specified as 1991 . One is the default value of PL/1 for the lower bound of an array. Bounds may be constants, variables, expressions, or asterisks. Bounds that are variables or expressions are determined when storage is allocated for the array. An asterisk means that the actual bounds are defined later, either in an ALLOCATE statement or via an argument to a subroutine or function procedure.

Since only the array itself is given a name, we reference an element of the array by means of a *subscript* (for this reason, array elements are often called *subscripted variables*). For example, to report the value of income for the year 1989, we might use PUT SKIP LIST(INCOME(1989));. Subscripts may be constants, variables, or *any* valid PL/1 arithmetic expression. The following program segment uses a DO loop to consecutively index the elements of an array:

```
LOOP: DO YEAR = 1981 TO 1991;
    PUT SKIP LIST('YEAR = ', YEAR, ' INCOME = ',
                                INCOME(YEAR));
END LOOP;
```

All the elements of an array can be set equal to a *scalar* (single) value by an assignment statement such as: INCOME = INCOME(1989);. Here, the value of the ninth element of the INCOME array is copied to each of the eleven positions of the INCOME array. It is also possible to copy (move) an array into another array, if the arrays have identical structures.

Arrays may also appear in arithmetic expressions. For example, the expression INCOME * 2 results in an array identical in structure to INCOME whose elements are twice the corresponding elements of INCOME. PL/1 supports matrix addition and subtraction but not matrix multiplication.

One method of loading data into an array is to use the *list-directed input,* GET LIST. For example, GET LIST(INCOME) will cause data to be entered into the array starting with the first item and continuing, element by element, until the data is exhausted. If the number of items read exceeds the number of elements in the array, the upper bound of the array will be exceeded and an error condition will be created. The following program segment uses this method of loading data into an array, but uses the *data-directed output,* PUT DATA, to print the array after sorting its elements in descending order.

```
/* Read 100 numbers and print them in descending order */
DECLARE NUMBER(100)    FIXED DECIMAL(2,0);
DECLARE TEMP           FIXED DECIMAL(2,0);
DECLARE (1, J)         FIXED BINARY;
GET LIST(NUMBER);
DO I = 1 TO 99;
   DO J = I+1 TO 100;
      IF NUMBER(I) < NUMBER(J)
      THEN DO;
           TEMP = NUMBER(I); NUMBER(I) = NUMBER(J);
                NUMBER(J) = TEMP;
      END;
   END;
END;
PUT DATA(NUMBER);
```

The following program segment represents a more efficient
sorting procedure. It also uses a *repetitive specification* for list-
directed input of a portion of the array.

```
/* Read up to 100 numbers and print them in ascending order */
DECLARE NUMBER(100)        FIXED DECIMAL(2,0);
DECLARE ACTUAL_COUNT       FIXED BINARY;
DECLARE TEMP               FIXED DECIMAL(2,0);
DECLARE I                  FIXED BINARY;
DECLARE SORTED             BIT(1);
DECLARE EXCHANGED          BIT(1);
DECLARE YES                BIT(1) INIT('1'B);
                           /* INITIAL abbreviated */
DECLARE NO                 BIT(1) INIT('0'B);

PUT LIST('How many numbers will be actually input?');
GET LIST(ACTUAL_COUNT);
GET LIST( (NUMBER(I) DO I = 1 TO ACTUAL_COUNT) );
/* read actual number of values */
```

39

```
SORTED = NO;
DO UNTIL (SORTED);
    EXCHANGED = NO;
    DO I = 1 TO ACTUAL_COUNT – 1;
        IF NUMBER(I) > NUMBER(I + 1)
        THEN DO;
            TEMP = NUMBER(I); NUMBER(I) = NUMBER(I+1);
                        NUMBER(I+1) = TEMP;
            EXCHANGED = YES;
        END;
    END;
    IF ^ EXCHANGED THEN SORTED = YES;
END;
```

5.2   MULTI-DIMENSIONAL ARRAYS

The number of sets of lower and upper bounds specifies the number of dimensions in an array. For example, the PL/1 declaration DECLARE INCOME(1981:1991, 4) FIXED DECIMAL(6);, defines a two-dimensional array which may be considered as a table containing income values for each quarter (second dimension of the array has an upper bound of 4 and a default lower bound of 1) of each year in the years 1981 through 1991 . The first dimension of a two-dimensional array refers to a row in the associated table, while the second dimension identifies a column. Thus, INCOME(1985, 3) refers to the element in the fifth row and the third column. By using an asterisk in place of a subscript, a *cross-section* of the array may be referenced. For example, the assignment statement INCOME(*, 3) = 0 will set the third quarter income for all the years to zero.

Appearance of a two-dimensional array name without subscripts in the list of a GET statement will cause values to be read in and assigned to the array, in *row-major order*. In other words, GET LIST(INCOME) will be equivalent to:

```
DO I = 1981 TO 1991;
    DO J = 1 TO 4;
        GET LIST(INCOME(I, J));
    END;
END;
```

Note that values for the whole two-dimensional array are always read; it is *not* possible to use this feature to read in part of the array.

When a multi-dimensional array is initialized using the INITIAL attribute, the initial values are also assigned in *row-major form*, that is, in such a way that the rightmost subscript varies most rapidly. For example, the following declaration DECLARE IDENTITY(5, 5) FIXED(5, 2) INITIAL ((5) (1, (5) 0)); would produce a 5 x 5 "identity" matrix. Here, the INITIAL specification uses two *iteration factors* of (5) to indicate that the values used to initialize the array consist of 1, 0, 0, 0, 0, 0 repeated five times. The same initialization would be accomplished by the following program segment:

```
IDENTITY = 0;
DO I = 1 TO 5; IDENTITY(I, I) = 1; END;
```

Although harder to visualize, arrays of higher dimensions may be declared and used in a similar fashion. For example, our income table may be expanded to store quarterly income of up to 50 different companies for the years 1981 to 1991 as follows: DECLARE INCOME(1981:1991, 4, 50) FIXED DECIMAL(6);. The program segment below determines the subscript (index) of the company with the highest single quarter income in 1989.

41

```
COMPANY_INDEX, QUARTER_INDEX = 1;
/* PL/1 multiple assignment statement */
HIGHEST_INCOME = INCOME(1989, QUARTER_INDEX,
                COMPANY_INDEX);
DO I = 1 TO 50;
   DO J = 1 TO 4;
      IF INCOME(1989, J, I) > HIGHEST_INCOME
      THEN DO;
         HIGHEST_INCOME = INCOME(1989, J, I);
         QUARTER_INDEX = J; COMPANY_INDEX = I;
      END;
   END;
END;
PUT SKIP LIST('Highest one quarter income: ',
              HIGHEST_INCOME);
PUT SKIP LIST('Achieved in quarter ', QUARTER INDEX, '
              by company # ', COMPANY_INDEX);
```

5.3   STRUCTURES

Arrays contain homogeneous data. Structures do not necessarily contain homogeneous data. A PL/1 structure is a collection of data organized into some sort of a hierarchy. The collection may be a mixture of character and numeric items – unlike
the collection of data organized by arrays that are required to
have the same attributes.

The PL/1 programmer tells the compiler that a data collection is a structure by means of a DECLARE statement such as:

```
DECLARE 1   CUSTOMER,
            2   NAME CHARACTER(25),
            2   HOME_ADDRESS,
                3   LINE(2)    CHARACTER(20),
                3   CITY       CHARACTER(15)
```

42

```
3  STATE      CHARACTER(2),
3  ZIP        FIXED DECIMAL(5),
2  BUSINESS_ADDRESS,
   3  LINE(2)    CHARACTER(20),
   3  CITY       CHARACTER(15)
   3  STATE      CHARACTER(2),
   3  ZIP        FIXED DECIMAL(5),
2  BALANCE FIXED DECIMAL(7,2);
```

Here, the numbers 1, 2, and 3 to the left of each identifier are referred to as *level numbers* and must be separated from the identifier by at least one blank. There is only one level 1 in each structure and its identifier is the name of the structure, CUSTOMER in this case. Any number greater than 1 may be used for subdivisions of the structure. Structure elements together with their attributes are separated by commas. Levels that are not further subdivided in a structure are called *elementary levels* and these are where data are actually stored.

In the case of CUSTOMER structure, identifiers NAME and BALANCE are at the elementary level 2 of the hierarchy and have attributes, since they represent data values. On the other hand, the identifiers HOME_ADDRESS and BUSINESS_ADDRESS are names of structures and hence do not have attributes since they do not represent a data value. While CUSTOMER is referred to as the *major structure,* HOME_ADDRESS and BUSINESS_ADDRESS are called *minor structures.*

Identifier LINE (intended to store first and second lines of an address) represents an array of *two* 20-character elements within the structures HOME_ADDRESS and BUSINESS_ADDRESS. If we wish to refer to the first line in an address, we refer to LINE(1), and if we need the second line we refer to it by LINE(2).

Identifiers LINE, CITY, STATE, and ZIP all appear at the elementary level 3 of the hierarchy and have attributes since they represent data values.

To refer to a data item in a structure, a *fully qualified* identifier may be used. For example, to print the home zip code we can use: PUT LIST(CUSTOMER.HOME_ADDRESS.ZIP);. The decimal point used in this context is called the *qualification operator.* Full qualification is not necessary if there is no risk of ambiguity. For example, identifier BALANCE appears only once in the structure and thus need not be fully qualified.

When writing programs involving structures, it is often necessary to declare several identifiers to have the same structure. This can be accomplished in PL/1 in a straightforward manner by using the LIKE attribute as follows:

```
DECLARE OLD_CUSTOMER LIKE CUSTOMER;
```

If a structure is used in an assignment statement, the receiving entry must also be a structure. Thus, OLD_CUSTOMER = CUSTOMER; and CUSTOMER.HOME_ADDRESS = OLD_CUSTOMER.BUSINESS_ADDRESS; are valid PL/1 statements. It is also possible to assign a scalar value to a structure, in which case an attempt is made to assign the scalar value to *every* data element in the structure. This may cause an error condition when the data elements are not homogeneous. Finally, structures may not be used in expressions, in particular, logical conditions such as in IF OLD_CUSTOMER = CUSTOMER THEN; are forbidden.

5.4   ARRAYS OF STRUCTURES

We have already indicated that it is possible to have arrays as structure elements (e.g., LINE in the HOME_ADDRESS structure). It is also possible to construct arrays in which each element is a structure. To start, below we re-declare CUSTOMER as a structure whose element ADDRESS is an array of two structures representing respectively the home and the business address of the customer.

```
DECLARE 1  CUSTOMER,
           2  NAME  CHARACTER(25),
           2  ADDRESS (2),
              3  LINE(2)   CHARACTER(20),
              3  CITY      CHARACTER(15)
              3  STATE     CHARACTER(2),
              3  ZIP       FIXED DECIMAL(5),
           2  BALANCE      FIXED DECIMAL(7,2);
```

As it can be seen, to declare an array of structures, a structure identifier – either major or minor – can be assigned the *dimension attribute*. The program segment below sorts an array of 1000 customers by their business address zip code value.

```
DECLARE CUSTOMERS(1000) LIKE CUSTOMER;
DECLARE TEMP LIKE CUSTOMER;
DO I = 1 TO 999;
    DO J = I+1 TO 1000;
        IF CUSTOMERS(I).ADDRESS(2).ZIP >
                        CUSTOMERS(J).ADDRESS(2).ZIP
        THEN DO;
            TEMP = CUSTOMER(I); CUSTOMER(I) =
                        CUSTOMER(J); CUSTOMER(J) = TEMP;
        END;
    END;
END;
```

```
/* Display the mailing list in order */
DO I = 1 TO 1000;
    PUT SKIP LIST(CUSTOMERS(I).NAME);
    PUT SKIP LIST(CUSTOMERS(I).ADDRESS(2).LINE(1));
    PUT SKIP LIST(CUSTOMERS(I).ADDRESS(2).LINE(2));
    PUT SKIP LIST(CUSTOMERS(I).ADDRESS(2).CITY);
    PUT SKIP LIST(CUSTOMERS(I).ADDRESS(2).STATE);
    PUT SKIP LIST(CUSTOMERS(I).ADDRESS(2).ZIP);
END;
```

The program segment below accomplishes the same objective more efficiently by avoiding the switching of elements of the CUSTOMERS array. Instead, an array, named TAGS, is constructed which contains subscripts of the CUSTOMERS array in the desired order.

```
DECLARE CUSTOMERS(1000) LIKE CUSTOMER;
DECLARE TAGS(1000) FIXED BINARY;
DECLARE TEMP FIXED BINARY;
DO I = 1 TO 1000;
    TAGS(I) = I;
END;
DO I = 1 TO 999;
    DO J = I+1 TO 1000;
        IF CUSTOMERS(TAGS(I)).ADDRESS(2).ZIP >
                CUSTOMERS(TAGS(J)).ADDRESS(2).ZIP
        THEN DO;
            TEMP = TAGS(I); TAGS(I) = TAGS(J); TAGS(J)
                = TEMP;
        END;
    END;
END;
```

```
/* Display the mailing list in order */
DO I = 1 TO 1000;
     PUT SKIP LIST(CUSTOMERS(TAGS(I)).NAME);
     PUT SKIP LIST(CUSTOMERS(TAGS(I)).ADDRESS(2).LINE(1));
     PUT SKIP LIST(CUSTOMERS(TAGS(I)).ADDRESS(2).LINE(2));
     PUT SKIP LIST(CUSTOMERS(TAGS(I)).ADDRESS(2).CITY);
     PUT SKIP LIST(CUSTOMERS(TAGS(I)).ADDRESS(2).STATE);
     PUT SKIP LIST(CUSTOMERS(TAGS(I)).ADDRESS(2).ZIP);
END;
```

CHAPTER 6

PROCEDURES

6.1 SUBROUTINE PROCEDURES

Built-in functions (or library functions) such as SQRT are used (or *called)* by simply writing them into expressions (e.g., A = SQRT(B);) as though they were variables. They return only one value to the *calling* program. Subroutines, on the other hand, can return any number of values. In PL/1, a subroutine procedure is *invoked* by the CALL statement, e.g., CALL ADD2(X, Y, Z), where X, Y, and Z are the data to be manipulated by the subroutine called the *argument list*. A program using subroutines consists of two kinds of procedures: a single main procedure and any number of subprograms (subroutines and functions). The main procedure identified by OPTIONS(MAIN), controls the flow to subprograms. The argument list in the CALL statement are two-way links to a similar series of *parameters* in the PROCEDURE statement of the subroutine. Consider the following example:

EXAMPLE: PROCEDURE OPTIONS(MAIN);
DECLARE X FIXED DECIMAL(7, 2);
DECLARE Y FIXED DECIMAL(7, 2);
DECLARE Z FIXED DECIMAL(8, 2);

```
GET LIST(X, Y);
CALL ADD2(X, Y, Z);
PUT LIST('The sum is: ', Z);
END EXAMPLE;

ADD2: PROCEDURE( A, B, C );
DECLARE A FIXED DECIMAL(7, 2);
DECLARE B FIXED DECIMAL(7, 2);
DECLARE C FIXED DECIMAL(8, 2);
C = A + B;
RETURN;
END ADD2;
```

Here, the subroutine ADD2 simply adds the two values passed to it through its first two parameters (A and B) and returns their sum through its third parameter (C). Any change in the value of a parameter in a subroutine will actually be a change in the value of the matching argument in the calling procedure. Such changes remain in effect when control is returned to the calling procedure. Therefore, when the PUT LIST statement is executed, the value of Z that will be printed will be the sum of X and Y.

The attributes of a parameter and its corresponding argument must be the same. If the attributes of an argument are not consistent with its corresponding parameter, an error will probably result, since *no conversion is automatically performed*. In general, an argument and its corresponding parameter need not be only variable names. They can be most data types including: numeric constants; bit strings; character strings; expressions; array names; array expressions; major or minor structure names; built-in function names; entry names; file names; and labels.

When a CALL statement is executed, control transfers from the calling procedure to the first executable statement in the

49

procedure named in the CALL statement. The statements in the called procedure are then executed until a RETURN statement or its END statement is encountered. At that point, control transfers back to the calling procedure and to the statement following the CALL statement. However, it is possible for the called procedure to contain a CALL statement to a third procedure and so on. Such *nesting* of procedure calls is permissible in PL/1 as long as *identifier scope* rules are obeyed.

A STOP or an EXIT statement in a subroutine abnormally terminates execution of that subroutine and of the entire program. It is a good practice to avoid this manner of terminating the program and instead provide for the subroutine to return an error indicator to the calling program. It should be the MAIN program's function to decide what action should be taken, and when necessary, to terminate the program prematurely.

For arguments that are bit or character strings, as well as for arrays, the corresponding parameters may be declared with an asterisk for the length attribute. The following procedure computes the mean, minimum, and the maximum value for an array of floating-point values.

```
MMM: PROCEDURE( A, MEAN, MIN, MAX );
DECLARE A(*) DECIMAL FLOAT;
/* The asterisk tells the compiler to align storage for the array A with
those of the actual array used in the calling statement */
DECLARE MEAN DECIMAL FLOAT;
DECLARE MIN DECIMAL FLOAT;
DECLARE MAX DECIMAL FLOAT;
DECLARE I FIXED BINARY;
N = HBOUND(A, 1);
/* The built-in function HBOUND finds the current upper bound for a
specified dimension of a given array */
MEAN, MIN, MAX = A(1); /* Initialize results */
```

```
DO I = 2 TO N;
    MEAN = MEAN + A(I);
    IF A(I) > MAX
    THEN MAX = A(I);
    ELSE IF A(I) < MIN THEN MIN = A(I);
END;
MEAN = MEAN / N;
END MMM;
```

6.2 INTERNAL SUBPROGRAMS, *EXTERNAL* VARIABLES, AND DUMMY ARGUMENTS

A subroutine procedure that is separately compiled from its calling (invoking) procedure is called an *external procedure*. The length of such procedures' names is limited to seven or eight characters. More importantly, however, identifiers declared in the procedure or appearing as formal parameters in the PROCEDURE statement have *no* relationship to any identifier used outside the procedure *unless* they are given the EXTERNAL attribute in *both* procedures. In the example below, both procedures share the variable COMMON. Had COMMON not been given the EXTERNAL attribute, each procedure would have had its own local variable named COMMON.

```
PROC1: PROCEDURE;
DECLARE COMMON FIXED BINARY EXTERNAL;
. . .


END PROC1;
PROC2: PROCEDURE;
DECLARE COMMON FIXED BINARY EXTERNAL;
. . .
END PROC2;
```

51

When a subprogram is placed inside the calling procedure, with the PROCEDURE statement of the subprogram after, and its END statement before the corresponding statements of the calling procedure, the subprogram is called an *internal procedure* and information may be passed between the calling procedure and the subprogram in other ways than with the use of parameters. For example, if the identifier Y is used in both the calling procedure and in an internal procedure, and Y is not declared in the internal procedure, then the same storage location is used for both Y's. Therefore, a change in Y inside the subprogram will affect the value stored for Y in the calling procedure.

In general, the range of statements which can reference an identifier is known as the identifier's *scope*. In PL/1, the rules governing scope of identifiers are such that an identifier may have only one meaning at any point in time. It is possible, however, for the same name to have different meanings in different parts of the program. Basically, the scope of a *declared* PL/1 identifier includes the entire procedure (or the BEGIN block) where it is declared. This includes all procedures which are internal to that procedure and which themselves do not contain declaration for that identifier. When an identifier is *undeclared*, its scope includes the procedure in which it is referenced, together with all procedures in which it is embedded that do not themselves declare that identifier. The two situations are depicted below:

```
PROG1: PROCEDURE OPTIONS(MAIN);
. . .
    PROC2: PROCEDURE;
    I = 1;
    . . .
    END PROC2;
. . .
END PROG1;
```

```
PROG2: PROCEDURE OPTIONS(MAIN) ;
. . .
     PROC3: PROCEDURE;
     DECLARE I FIXED BINARY;

     . . .
     PROC4: PROCEDURE;
     /* Assume I is not declared in this procedure */

     . . .
     END PROC4;
     . . .
     END PROC3;
. . .
END PROG2;
```

In PROG1, identifier I is not explicitly declared and as such its scope will be the entire program. References to I anywhere in PROG1 affect the same storage location. In PROG2, identifier I is declared in procedure PROC3, and thus its scope is delimited to the entire procedure including PROC4. References to I in the main program will affect a different storage location.

We conclude this section by examining somewhat more closely the PL/1 conventions for associating parameters with arguments at the time of invocation of subprograms. When an argument agrees in all attributes with its corresponding parameter, it is associated by reference (address) with the parameter. This means that all references to the parameter within the procedure directly use the actual storage location of the argument. This method of data transmission to a subprogram is known as *call by reference.*

If an argument disagrees in any of its attributes with its corresponding parameter, a so-called dummy argument with the same value is created and used throughout the invocation of the procedure. Since the dummy argument is in a separate storage location than the storage location for the actual argument, the value of the original argument will not be affected by the invocation of the subprogram. This method of data transmission is named *call by value* and is only acceptable for arguments which are used strictly as input to the procedure. For arguments that are intended to serve as output from the procedure, call being a reference is a necessary requirement.

Finally, if the argument is not a simple variable name then a dummy argument is automatically created at the time of invocation of the subprogram.

6.3   FUNCTION PROCEDURES

A function is a procedure that returns a single value to the calling procedure. The value returned may not be an aggregate, i.e., an array or a structure. A function is invoked in the same manner that PL/1 built-in functions are referenced. Functions should not be invoked by a CALL, nor should subroutines be invoked by a function reference.

The RETURN statement is used to terminate a function. Its use in a function differs from its use in a subroutine. In a function, the RETURN statement has an argument. The value of the *expression* in RETURN will be assigned to the name of the function in the calling procedure. One RETURN statement is, thus, always needed in a function subprogram. However, there may be more than one RETURN statement in a function, the execution of any one of which will transfer control back to the procedure that invoked the function.

We have already indicated that it is very important to insure that the attributes of arguments be the same as those of the matching parameters in the called procedure. When writing a function, an additional consideration is the attributes of the value returned by the function. If the attributes of the value returned by a function are different from those expected by the calling procedure, errors will result. Consider, as an example, the rewriting of the subroutine ADD2 which happens to return a single value as a function:

```
ADD2: PROCEDURE( A, B );
DECLARE A FIXED DECIMAL(7, 2);
DECLARE B FIXED DECIMAL(7, 2);
RETURN( A + B );
END ADD2;
```

When the programmer uses the function ADD2 in a statement such as $Z = ADD2(X, Y)$;, the PL/1 compiler needs to know the attributes of the result returned by ADD2 so that proper conversion instructions may be generated to convert the result data to the data format of the variable W. The attributes of returned values from functions may be decided either by default (according to the first letter of the function name) or by using the RETURNS *option*. In the latter case, both the calling procedure and the function include the RETURNS keyword as follows:

```
MAIN: PROCEDURE OPTIONS(MAIN);
DECLARE ADD2 ENTRY RETURNS(FIXED DECIMAL(8));
DECLARE X FIXED DECIMAL(7, 2);
DECLARE Y FIXED DECIMAL(7, 2);
. . .
W = ADD2( X, Y );
. . .
END MAIN;

ADD2: PROCEDURE( A, B ) RETURNS(FIXED DECIMAL(8));
DECLARE A FIXED DECIMAL(7, 2);
DECLARE B FIXED DECIMAL(7, 2);
RETURN( A + B );
END ADD2;
```

55

The *ENTRY attribute* of the DECLARE statement in the calling procedure (see line 2) allows the programmer to direct the PL/1 compiler to generate appropriate code for conversion of one or more arguments to match the attributes of their corresponding parameters, should arguments and their associated parameters have different attributes. For example, in the previous program segment, if X and Y are declared to be in floating-point format an error would result since they would not have the same attributes as their corresponding parameters A and B. However, using the ENTRY attribute in the explicit declaration of the ADD2 function (DECLARE ADD2 ENTRY(FIXED DECIMAL(7,2), FIXED DECIMAL(7,2)) RETURNS(FIXED DECIMAL(8);) obviates the error by directing the PL/1 compiler to generate the necessary conversion code from floating-point to fixed decimal.

Occasionally, it is desirable to use a subprogram (subroutine or function) in two ways, the second way requiring only part of the entire subprogram. For example, suppose we needed functions to compute the area of a triangle in inches squared and centimeters squared given the length of its three sides in inches. The following program segment illustrates the use of the *ENTRY statement* which allows us to have two labels in one procedure which can be used to invoke the procedure from outside.

```
. . .
PUT SKIP LIST('Enter the length of each side in inches?');
GET LIST( X, Y, Z );
PUT SKIP LIST('Area in inches squared is: ', AREA_INCH(X, Y, Z));
PUT SKIP LIST('Area in centimeters squared is: ',
                  AREA_CENTIMETER(X, Y, Z));
. . .
```

```
AREA_CENTIMETER: PROCEDURE( A, B, C );
A= A * 2.54; B = B * 2.54; C = C * 2.54;
/* covert sides, 1 inch = 2.54 centimeter */
AREA_INCH: ENTRY( A, B, C );
/* Area = SQRT( S (S − A) ( S − B) (S − C) ),
where S = (A + B + C) /2 */
S = (A + B + C) /2;
AREA = SQRT(S*(S − A)*(S − B)*(S − C));
RETURN(AREA);
END AREA_CENTIMETER;
```

6.4 RECURSIVE PROCEDURES

A recursive procedure is one that will invoke itself. In other words, the procedure calls upon itself. In PL/1, the keyword RECURSIVE is used to indicate the use of the recursive option as shown in the following example:

```
/* Given N >= 1. If N = 1 then Factorial(N) = 1 else Factorial(N) = N *
Factorial(N - 1) */
FACTORIAL: PROCEDURE(N) RETURNS(FIXED BINARY)
                    RECURSIVE;
    DECLARE N FIXED BINARY;
    IF N = 1 THEN RETURN(N);
                    ELSE RETURN(N * FACTORIAL(N − 1));
END FACTORIAL;
```

CHAPTER 7

STREAM I/O

7.1 FILE DECLARATIONS

A collection of data stored on punched cards, magnetic tape, or disk is termed a *data set*. A collection of data fields, such as those encountered in relation to employees' payroll data (employee ID, name, hourly rate, etc.), is termed a record, or, more precisely, a *logical record* because the distinct data fields have a logical relationship to one another. A grouping of logical records is termed a *file*, which may be viewed independently of the physical properties of a data set and the storage medium on which it is stored.

In PL/1, input and output operations are performed against files. For example, the statement GET LIST(A); is, in fact, equivalent to GET FILE(SYSIN) LIST(A);, where SYSIN is the identifier for the *standard input file*. Similarly, the statement PUT LIST(A); is, in fact, equivalent to PUT FILE(SYSPRINT) LIST(A);, where SYSPRINT identifies the *standard output file*. When file names are omitted from a GET or PUT, default file names are assumed.

The SYSIN and SYSPRINT file names do not have to be

explicitly declared. For other files, however, the programmer must declare a file name and a set of *file attributes*. The attributes provide information on the physical characteristics of the file and the method of using the associated data set. For example, the declaration DECLARE MYFILE RECORD OUTPUT SEQUENTIAL BUFFERED; specifies that the file MYFILE is to be treated as a sequence of records (record I/O), that the file will be written to, that the file is organized and accessed sequentially, and that the records transmitted between the external storage medium and a specified location in the program's memory must pass through a buffer (which allows input and output to be overlapped with processing).

As with data attributes, file attributes can be declared explicitly, contextually, or implicitly. The attributes that apply to stream I/O are as follows: FILE; STREAM; INPUT or OUTPUT; PRINT; and ENVIRONMENT. For example, the default declarations for SYSIN have the following attributes: FILE STREAM INPUT ENVIRONMENT(F BLKSIZE(80)), which defines SYSIN as a stream-oriented input file of fixed-length records that are 80 characters long.

Several programming steps are required when input and operations are specified. The first step is to declare the file and specify its attributes. The second step is to open the file. STREAM files, such as SYSIN, are automatically opened when the first GET or PUT to that file is issued. The third step is to process information in the file using READ or WRITE statements (record I/O) or GET or PUT statements (stream I/O). The final step is to close the file.

The program in Figure 3 demonstrates the essential principles by creating a disk file of names and addresses input from the terminal (standard input file).

7.2   LIST-DIRECTED I/O

In list-directed I/O, which uses the LIST keyword, the input stream is a list of valid constants, separated by blanks or commas. The output stream is a series of data values, each separated by a blank. The format of each data item is determined by the attributes of the associated variable. List-directed I/O uses the data conversion specifications for *arithmetic to character* and *character to arithmetic* conversions. The program segment below, when used with the input data "12, 34.5 'LIST-DI-RECTED I/O'" will result in "12.00 3.45000E+01 LIST-DI-RECTED I/O" to be printed in the first three print zones of the output line (each zone is 24 columns wide).

```
DECLARE A DECIMAL FIXED(4,2);
DECLARE B FLOAT(6);
DECLARE C CHARACTER(17);
GET FILE(SYSIN) LIST(A, B, C);
PUT FILE(SYSPRINT) LIST(A, B, C);
```

When the PRINT attribute is specified for stream files, it indicates that the file is to be printed on a line printer. The PRINT attribute causes the initial byte of each record of the associated data set to be reserved for a printer control character. This printer control character is appropriately set when the *options* SKIP, LINE, or PAGE are used in the PUT statement. The PAGE option of the PUT statement is used to cause a page ejection, while the LINE option specifies the actual line on the page where the data is to be printed. And, the SKIP option is used to start printing at the beginning of the next line regardless of whether the keyword SKIP is used before LIST (e.g., PUT SKIP LIST('A new line.');) or after the data list (i.e., PUT LIST('A new line.') SKIP;).

7.3 DATA-DIRECTED I/O

In data-directed I/O, which uses the DATA keyword, the input stream is a sequence of valid assignments of the form, v = c, where c is a valid constant, and v is the variable to which it is assigned. Assignments must be separated by a blank or comma, and those for each GET statement *must* be terminated

```
PRGRM3: PROCEDURE OPTIONS(MAIN);
DECLARE DISKFILE FILE STREAM OUTPUT
                ENVIRONMENT(F RECSIZE(40) BLKSIZE(40));
DECLARE FILENAME CHARACTER(8) VARYING;
DECLARE NAME CHARACTER(20) VARYING;
DECLARE ADDRESS CHARACTER(30) VARYING;
DECLARE RESPONSE CHARACTER(1);
DECLARE MORE_DATA BIT(1);
DECLARE YES BIT(1) INIT('1'B);
DECLARE NO BIT(1) INIT('0'B);

PUT SKIP LIST('Enter the output filename?');
GET LIST(FILENAME);
OPEN FILE(DISKFILE) TITLE(FILENAME);
/* filename in a job control statement */
MORE_DATA = YES;
DO WHILE (MORE_DATA);
    PUT SKIP LIST('Enter name?'); GET LIST(NAME);
    PUT SKIP LIST('Enter address?'); GET LIST(ADDRESS);

    PUT FILE(DISKFILE) LIST(NAME, ADDRESS);
    /* write to disk */

    PUT SKIP LIST('More data (Y/N)?'); GET LIST(RESPONSE);
    IF RESPONSE = 'Y' THEN; ELSE MORE_DATA = NO;
END;

CLOSE FILE(DISKFILE);
END PRGRM3;
```

Figure 3

61

by a semicolon. The input process is effectively reversed for data directed output. The program segment below when used with the input data "A=12, B = 34.5 C = 'DATA-DIRECTED I/O';" will result in "A = 12.00 B = 3.45000E+01 C = 'DATA-DIRECTED I/O';" to be printed in the first three print zones of the output line.

```
DECLARE A DECIMAL FIXED(4,2);
DECLARE B FLOAT(6);
DECLARE C CHARACTER(17);
GET FILE(SYSIN) DATA(A, B, C);
PUT FILE(SYSPRINT) DATA(A, B, C);
```

It is not an error for the data list in the GET DATA statement to include names (identifiers) that do not appear in the input stream. However, it is an error if there is an identifier in the input stream but not in the data list. Such an error raises the *NAME condition,* which may be handled in your program in the same manner as with other units (for example, ON NAME(SYSIN) BEGIN; ... END;);

It is also possible to exclude the data list from the GET DATA statement. In that case, the variables in the input stream may be any identifier known at that point in the program. The data list in the GET DATA statement is optional because a semicolon signals the end of the number of values to be obtained from the input stream.

It is also possible to specify PUT DATA;, in which case the values of all variables known to the program at that point will be output. This is a powerful debugging aid.

7.4   EDIT-DIRECTED I/O

In edit-directed I/O, which uses the EDIT keyword, input and output conversion is controlled by a *format list* that directs the manner in which conversion is performed. Data in the input and output streams are a continuous string of characters. There is no requirement to put single quote marks around character strings to be input, or to place blanks or commas between the input items. And, we are no longer restricted to print our results starting in the predefined print zones.

Each edit-directed input (GET) or output (PUT) statement contains not only the list of data items to be transmitted but also a list of format specifications for each data item. If there are more format specifications than data items, the extra specifications will be ignored. On the other hand, if the format list is exhausted before finishing reading (or writing) a data list, the format list will be reused for the remaining data items.

Our running example is depicted below using edit-directed I/O:

```
DECLARE A DECIMAL FIXED(4,2);
DECLARE B FLOAT(6);
DECLARE C CHARACTER(17);
GET FILE(SYSIN) EDIT(A, B, C) (X(5), F(3,1), X(2),
                  E(8,3), X(5), A(17));;
PUT FILE(SYSPRINT) EDIT(A, B, C) (R(FORMAT1));
FORMAT1: FORMAT(F(5,2), X(3), E(12,5), X(2), A);
```

Here, the format list of the GET statement specifies that the next 5 characters in the input stream are to be ignored (X(5)), the next 3 characters are to be read as a fixed point number and if the decimal point does not actually appear to use 1 digit as the fractional part (F(3,1)), the next two characters are to be ignored (X(2)), the next 8 characters are to be read as a floating-point number written in scientific notation with 3 digits to the right of the decimal point, if the decimal point does not actually appear (E(8,3)), the next 5 characters are to be ignored (X(5)), and finally the next 20 characters are to be read as a character string (A(20)).

The PUT EDIT statement in our example uses a *remote format list* identified by label FORMAT1. The use of remote format lists is one good programming practice, especially since one remote format may refer to another (e.g., FORMAT (SKIP, R(FORMAT1));). In the remote format statement FORMAT1, the A format specification for variable C does not specify a size for the output character string. This is permissible when we wish the entire character string to be printed. Given the following input, "!!!!!!120!!0.345E+2!!!!!!EDIT-DIRECTED I/O", the program will output, "12.00!!! 3.45000E+01!!EDIT-DIRECTED I/O", where we have used ! to denote a blank space.

With edit-directed output, the print control options SKIP, PAGE, and LINE may be used. It is also possible to begin printing in a specific column, say 10, as in PUT FILE(SYSPRINT) EDIT(COLUMN(10));. The COLUMN option may also be used with GET EDIT.

We conclude this section by mentioning two error *conditions* that could occur during input and output operations with stream files. The SIZE condition occurs during output if the width specification for a fixed binary or fixed decimal number is not large enough to contain the total value. For example, if the variable VALUE has the value -123, then the statement PUT EDIT(VALUE) (F(3)); will raise the SIZE condition. To print VALUE, a minimum field width of four columns is needed. As such, according to the rules of PL/1, the output field is *undefined*. Some PL/1 compilers generate code that fills the output field with asterisks; others may generate code that will truncate the value. A second condition, the CONVERSION condition, is raised if the input data includes illegal characters for the type of data item declared. For example, the data "12 34" input by the statement GET EDIT(VALUE) (COLUMN(1), F(5)); causes the CONVERSION condition to be raised since a blank appears in the *middle* of a numeric value. (A leading blank in a numeric field is treated as zero while trailing blanks are ignored.)

CHAPTER 8

RECORD I/O

8.1 RECORD VERSUS STREAM I/O

In record I/O, input or output is performed without data conversion. Computers use two ways to represent data electronically – an internal form used for storage in primary and secondary memory and an external character form used by the card reader (SYSIN) and printer (SYSPRINT). Data must be converted from one form to the other for transmission between card reader and main memory and back again for transmission between main memory and printer. On secondary storage (tapes and disks), data may be stored in either form. Stream files always use the external character form while record files always use the internal representation of data. GET and PUT statements are required when data conversion is necessary, as with stream files. READ and WRITE statements are used when no conversion is wanted, as with record files.

In stream I/O, data read is assigned to an arbitrary number of variables specified in the data list of the GET statement. In record I/O, data must be read as a single variable. Only one variable may be transmitted by each READ and WRITE statement. The attributes of the variable determine the record length transmitted. In general, the variable used for record I/O is declared as a major structure.

8.2 RECORD I/O STATEMENTS

Figure 4 presents a simple program which illustrates the various record I/O statements. The program is intended to read a deck of data cards each of which contains data in the following format: NAME in columns 1-25; ADDRESS in columns 26-50; CITY in columns 51-75; and ZIP CODE in columns 76-80. Each record read is to be printed, triple spaced, with 5 spaces between the output fields. The following annotations refer to the line numbers in Figure 4, which are not part of the actual program.

1.	PRGRM4: PROCEDURE OPTIONS(MAIN);
2.	DECLARE READER FILE RECORD INPUT SEQUENTIAL
	ENVIRONMENT(F RECSIZE(80) BLKSIZE(80));
3.	DECLARE WRITER FILE RECORD OUTPUT SEQUENTIAL
	ENVIRONMENT(F RECSIZE(133) CTLASA));
4.	DECLARE 1 CARD_IN,
4a.	3 NAME CHAR(25),
4b.	3 ADDRESS CHAR(25),
4c.	3 CITY_STATE CHAR(25),
4d.	3 ZIP_CODE CHAR(5);
5.	DECLARE 1 PRINT_OUT,
5a.	5 PRINTER_CONTROL CHAR(1) INIT('1'),
5b.	5 NAME CHAR(25)
5c.	5 FILLER_1 CHAR(5) INIT(' '),
5d.	5 ADDRESS CHAR(25),
5e.	5 FILLER 2 CHAR(5) INIT(' '),
5f.	5 CITY_STATE CHAR(25),
5g.	5 FILLER_3 CHAR(5) INIT(' '),
5h.	5 ZIP_CODE CHAR(25),
5i.	5 FILLER_4 CHAR(37) INIT(' '),

```
6.      DECLARE MORE_RECORDS CHAR(3) INIT('YES');

7.      ON ENDFILE(READER) MORE_RECORDS = 'No ';
8.      OPEN FILE(READER);
9.      OPEN FILE(WRITER);

10.     READ FILE(READER) INTO (CARD_IN);

11.     DO WHILE (MORE_RECORDS = 'YES');
12.         PRINT_OUT = CARD_IN, BY NAME;
13.         WRITE FILE(WRITER) FROM (PRINT_OUT);

14.     READ FILE(READER) INTO (CARD_IN);
15.     PRINT_CONTROL = '-';
16.     END;

17.     CLOSE FILE(READER), FILE(WRITER);

18.     END PRGRM4;
```

Figure 4

Line 1. Program PROCEDURE statement.

Line 2. The declaration of the file named READER as a sequential record file to be used for input. READER is also declared to have a fixed length record format of 80 bytes and is unblocked (i.e.. BLKSIZE = 1 * RECSIZE).

Line 3. The declaration of the file named WRITER as a sequential record file to be used for output. WRITER is also declared to have a fixed length record format of 133 bytes. The keyword CTLASA indicates that the first byte of each output record is the carriage control character.

Line 4-4d. Declaration of variable CARD_IN as a major structure consisting of four character string fields with a total length of 80 bytes.

Line 5-5i. Declaration of variable PRINT_OUT as a major structure with a total length of 133 bytes. (Note that it is permissible for two different structure variables (e.g., CARD_IN and PRINT_OUT) to share the same identifier (e.g., CITY_STATE) for their elementary items.) The PRINTER_CONTROL elementary item is initialized to '1' to provide for initial spacing to the top of the next page. Finally, note that PL/1 does not have a feature comparable to FILLER in COBOL to indicate unused space in the output record. As such, identifiers FILLER_1, FILLER_2, etc., must be defined and initialized to blanks.

Line 6. The character string variable MORE_RECORDS is declared and initialized to 'YES'.

Line 7. An on-unit is specified for when the ENDFILE condition is encountered with the READER file. The action to be taken is specified to be the assignment of the character string constant 'NO ' to the variable MORE_RECORDS.

Line 8-9. All files must be opened before a READ or WRITE can be issued to them.

Line 10. The READ statement will read the *next* record from the input file, READER, into program variable CARD_IN. Since the file READER had just been OPENed, the READ statement will input the very first record from the file.

Line 11. A DO WHILE loop begins here and ends with the END in line 16. The logical expression, MORE_RECORDS = 'YES", which controls the loop will evaluate to true since MORE_RECORDS was initialized to 'YES' in line 6. How-

69

ever, this will be true if and only if the READ statement in line 10 has not encountered an empty READER file.

Line 12. This assignment statement uses structure assignment *BY NAME*. The elementary items and minor structures of the structure variable CARD_IN are copied to identically named elementary items and minor structures of the structure variable PRINT_OUT. In this case, all four elementary items of CARD_IN (i.e., NAME, ADDRESS, CITY_STATE, and ZIP_CODE) are copied. Notice that the difference in level numbers (3 v. 5) is unimportant, only the hierarchical structuring is of concern.

Line 13. The WRITE statement copies the variable PRINT_OUT into the output file, WRITER.

Line 14. The READ statement attempts to read the next record from the input file, READER, into the program variable CARD_IN. Again, an end of file condition may result from this statement in which case control transfers to the programmer specified on-unit (line 7) before returning to the following statement.

Line 15. In preparation for printing out the next record, the carriage control character of the output record is initialized to '–' which is the CTLASA code for spacing three lines before printing.

Line 16. The end for the body of the loop which started in line 11 . The loop will terminate if MORE_RECORDS has been set to 'NO ', which can only occur as a result of an end of file condition. Otherwise, another iteration will begin with line 12.

Line 17. All files should be CLOSEd when processing is completed. Note that the CLOSE statement (like the OPEN statement) can specify more than one file.

Line 18. End of the program labeled PRGRM4.

8.3 *PICTURE* SPECIFICATION

There are several reasons for using PICTURE data including: to treat character strings as numeric values and vice versa; to edit data (e.g., include currency symbols); and to validate data (e.g., requiring presence of digits in specific positions).

A *character string picture specification* is a means of describing a fixed length character string and employs the following *PICTURE characters: X,* specifies that the associated character position can be occupied by any character from the character set; A, specifies that the associated character position can be occupied by any alphabetic or blank character; 9, specifies that the associated character position can be occupied by a decimal digit or a blank. The character string PICTURE attribute is primarily used for data validation. For example, given the declaration, DECLARE ITEM_CODE PICTURE '999AA9';, the assignment of '123XYZ' to ITEM_NUMBER will raise the CONVERSION condition since the last character of any ITEM_CODE is specified to be one of the digits 0-9.

A *numeric character picture specification* gives the format of a numeric data item that is stored in character form. That picture specification will be used to convert the data to a computational form prior to computation and back again when the data is to be stored. The following *PICTURE characters* are used to specify digits and decimal points: 9, specifies that the associated character position contains a decimal digit; V, specifies an *implied* decimal point at that position in the data item. For example, given the declaration DECLARE A PICTURE '999V99'; and A = 12.3;, then A contains the characters "01230". Note that the V character does not occupy a character position in the data item.

71

Zero suppression PICTURE characters specify digit positions that are conditionally replaced by blanks or asterisks: Z, specifies that a leading zero is to be replaced by a blank; *, specifies that a leading zero is to be replaced by an asterisk; Y, specifies that a zero (leading or non-leading) is to be replaced by a blank. For example, given the declaration DECLARE A PICTURE '****.V99', B PICTURE 'ZZZ9.V99', C PICTURE 'ZZZ9.V9Y'; and A, B, C = 12.3;, then A contains the characters "**12.30", B contains "!!12.30", and C contains "!!12.3!".

Insertion PICTURE characters denote that specific characters are to be inserted into the associated position of the character string value of a numeric character data item. Insertion characters include comma (,) and point (.) which are inserted into the specified character position only when no zero suppression occurs for the digit to the left of the comma or point position. For example, given the declaration DECLARE A PICTURE 'Z,ZZZ,ZZ9V.99'; and A = 1234.56;, then A contains "!!!!!1,234.56". Note that because the V does not automatically cause printing of a point, the point character must immediately precede or follow the V in a picture specification. If the point precedes the V, then the point will be inserted only if a significant digit appears to the left of the implied decimal point. If the point follows the V, then it will be suppressed only if all digits to the right of the implied decimal point are suppressed.

Sign and currency PICTURE characters can cause zero suppression if more than one of them is used. For example, given the declaration DECLARE A PICTURE '$Z,ZZZ,ZZ9V.99', B PICTURE '$$,$$$,$$9.V99', C PICTURE '++,+++.V99'; and A = 123.45; B = 12345; C = – 12.3;, then A contains "$!!!!!!123.45", B contains "!!!!!12,345.00", and C contains "!!!!!!1.23".

CHAPTER 9

STORAGE CLASSES AND LIST PROCESSING

9.1 *BEGIN* BLOCKS

Consider the following program segment:

```
DECLARE A(1000) FIXED DECIMAL(5,2);
DECLARE ACTUAL_COUNT FIXED BINARY;
GET LIST(ACTUAL_COUNT);
GET LIST(A(I) DO I = 1 TO ACTUAL_COUNT);
. . .
```

Here, because we are not sure of how many numbers will actually be input, we have declared the array to contain more elements than we think we would ever need. Then, when the program is run, we obtain the actual count from the user and read in only the actual number of data values. This could obviously result in wasting a lot of storage space. However, because we cannot predict the actual number of input values from one execution of the program to the next, it appears to be our only choice.

A second problem with the above approach occurs when

the program is used to input more than 1000 data values. In that case, because the implied DO loop will reference a location outside the bounds of the array, the SUBSCRIPTRANGE error condition will be raised if it has been enabled.

To overcome these disadvantages, PL/1 offers the programmer the BEGIN block which is used to allocate storage *dynamically*. Consider the rewriting of the previous program segment using a BEGIN block:

```
DECLARE ACTUAL_COUNT FIXED BINARY;
GET LIST(ACTUAL_COUNT);
BEGIN;
    DECLARE A(ACTUAL_COUNT) FIXED DECIMAL(5,2);
    GET LIST(A);
    . . .
END;
```

Here, storage for the array A is not set aside until the BEGIN block is actually entered during execution at which point the exact value of ACTUAL_COUNT is already known. After the BEGIN block has been executed, the storage locations for the array A are released in an *automatic* fashion.

BEGIN blocks can be nested just like DO loops or procedures. You cannot transfer into the middle of a BEGIN block, but you can transfer out from within. BEGIN blocks and procedure (blocks) share similar rules for scope of identifiers. Also, the dynamic allocation of storage applies to procedure (blocks) as well as BEGIN blocks.

9.2 *AUTOMATIC* STORAGE

Associated with each variable in PL/1 is the *storage class attribute* that effectively determines when main storage for that variable is allocated. Storage for a variable that has the AUTO-MATIC attribute is allocated when the procedure or BEGIN block in which that variable is declared is entered during execution. Storage for that variable remains allocated until that block is terminated; at that time, storage for the variable is released and any value that is stored there is lost. In PL/1, variables are given the AUTOMATIC attribute by default unless the variable has been given the EXTERNAL scope attribute.

9.3 *STATIC* STORAGE

Storage for variables with STATIC attribute is allocated when the program is loaded into main storage and remains allocated until the program is terminated. The STATIC attribute is of limited use since it only means that the storage and attributes of the variable are established on a permanent basis, but it does not mean that the variable is known outside the procedure or BEGIN block in which it is defined. If you want to use the same storage location for a variable regardless of where it appears in the program and want it to be known in several blocks external to each other, you may declare it to have the same attributes in each of the blocks and in addition give it the EXTERNAL scope attribute in each case. The PL/1 compiler assumes the STATIC attribute for variables with the EXTERNAL scope attribute.

The sample programs below illustrate the difference between AUTOMATIC and STATIC storage classes. The output of sample program AUTO will consist of five ones, while sample program STATIC will output numbers 1 through 5.

```
AUTO: PROCEDURE OPTIONS(MAIN);
DO I = 1 TO 5;
```

```
    CALL SUBROUTINE;
END;

SUBROUTINE: PROCEDURE;
DECLARE J INITIAL(1);
PUT LIST(J);
J = J + 1;
RETURN;
END SUBROUTINE;

END AUTO;

STATIC: PROCEDURE OPTIONS(MAIN);
DO I = 1 TO 5;
    CALL SUBROUTINE;
END;

SUBROUTINE: PROCEDURE;
DECLARE J STATIC INITIAL(1);
PUT LIST(J);
J = J + 1;
RETURN;
END SUBROUTINE;

END STATIC;
```

9.4 *CONTROLLED* STORAGE

The CONTROLLED storage class passes responsibility for allocating and freeing a variable's storage to the programmer. Storage is allocated when an ALLOCATE statement specifying that variable is executed and remains allocated until a FREE statement specifying that variable is executed. Storage allocated with the ALLOCATE statement remains allocated even after the block containing the variable declaration and the AL-

LOCATE statement may have been terminated. As such, it is possible to allocate a new *instance* of the controlled variable before the old version is freed. A reference to a controlled variable always refers to that instance of the variable which

---

```
PRGRM5: PROCEDURE OPTIONS(MAIN);
PUT LIST('How many numbers will be input?');
GET LIST(K);

DO I = 1 TO K;
    GET LIST(N);
    CALL PUSH(N);
END;

PUT SKIP LIST('The numbers in reverse order of input:');

DO I = 1 TO K;
    CALL POP(N);
    PUT SKIP LIST(N);
END;

PUSH: PROCEDURE(NUMBER);
DECLARE M CONTROLLED;
ALLOCATE M;
M = NUMBER;
RETURN;
POP: ENTRY(NUMBER); /* MULTIPLE ENTRY PROCEDURE */
NUMBER = M;
FREE M;
RETURN;
END PUSH;

END PRGRM5;
```

Figure 5

---

was most recently allocated. The next most recently allocated instance becomes accessible only after a FREE statement specifying the controlled variable is executed. Therefore, a series of allocations for the same variable creates a last-in first-out stack. This is demonstrated by the program in Figure 5 which inputs a series of numbers and prints them out in reverse order of input.

9.5 *BASED* STORAGE

The BASED storage class is similar to the CONTROLLED storage class, with the exception that all instances of a based variable may be referenced at any time during program execution. The mechanism for referencing the different instances of a based variable is provided by the concept of *pointer variables*. BASED storage is allocated with the ALLOCATE statement, and at the same time, a pointer variable is set to point to the location of the allocated storage. For example, given the declaration DECLARE Y BASED(P);, the execution of ALLOCATE Y; causes storage to be allocated for Y and, at the same time, pointer variable P (called the based variable's *home pointer)* is set to point to (i.e., contain the address of) the storage location of Y. By saving the value of P in another pointer variable, say Q, it becomes possible to refer to this instance of Y by Q –> Y (known as a *locator qualifier),* even after execution of a subsequent ALLOCATE Y; statement. This is demonstrated in the following program segment:

```
DECLARE Y BASED(P);
DECLARE Q POINTER;
ALLOCATE Y; Y = 1.00;
/* P now points to the storage location containing value 1.00 */
Q = P;
ALLOCATE Y; Y = 2.00;
/* P now points to the storage location containing value 1.00 */
```

PUT SKIP LIST(Y); /* Prints the value 2.00 */
PUT SKIP LIST(P –> Y); /* Prints the value 2.00 */
PUT SKIP LIST(Q –> Y); /* Prints the value 1.00 */
ALLOCATE Y SET(R);
/* Allocates storage for Y and sets the implicitly declared pointer
variable R to point to it. P still points to the last instance of Y. */
Y = 3.00;
R –> Y = 4.00;
PUT SKIP LIST(Y); /* Prints the value 3.00 */
PUT SKIP LIST(R –> Y);
/* Prints the value 4.00 */
FREE Y;
PUT SKIP LIST(Y);
/* Prints the value 2.00 */

Finally, the storage address of any program variable may be obtained from the built-in function ADDR. Among other things, this allows the programmer to use the same storage area for two different variables. Normally, the DEFINED attribute can be used to *overlay* one storage area on another. For example, the declarations DECLARE A(100) FIXED BINARY(15); and DECLARE B(50) FIXED BINARY(15) DEFINED A; result in arrays A and B to occupy the same storage area. However, a restriction of the DEFINED attribute is that only identifiers of the same base, scale, and precision may be overlayed. If there is a need to overlay variables with different attributes a technique similar to the following example may be used:

DECLARE ARRAY1(100) FLOAT DECIMAL(6);
DECLARE ARRAY2(70) FIXED BINARY(15)
                BASED(ARRAY2_POINTER);
. . .
ARRAY2_POINTER = ADDR(ARRAY1);

9.6 *LIST* PROCESSING

A *linked list* is a data structure with elements that do not necessarily occupy consecutive storage locations. An element of a linked list, frequently referred to as a *node,* is a structure variable of which one elementary item is a pointer variable. The pointer variable in each node is used to point to the next node in the list. The built-in function NULL can be used to set the pointer value in the last node. Normally, the first element of the list is pointed to by a scalar variable of type POINTER.

Figure 6 presents a program to illustrate list processing in PL/1. The program is intended to read a series of names and to print them in alphabetical order. The data structure used is a linked list. As each name is input, a node containing the name is created and placed in its proper (alphabetical) place in the list.

```
PRGRM6; PROCEDURE OPTIONS(MAIN);
DECLARE 1 NODE BASED(P),
                2 NAME CHARACTER(30),
                2 LINK POINTER;
DECLARE (HEAD,  CURRENT, LAST) POINTER;
/* Note factoring of identifiers */
DECLARE NULL BUILTIN;
/* Built-in functions that do not have arguments must be
declared */
DECLARE INPUT CHARACTER(30);
DECLARE MORE_DATA BIT(1) INITIAL('1'B');
DECLARE YES BIT(1) INITIAL('1'B);
DECLARE NO BIT(1) INITIAL('0'B);
DECLARE INSERTED BIT(1);

ON ENDFILE(SYSIN) MORE_DATA = NO;
```

```
HEAD = NULL;
GET LIST(INPUT);
DO WHILE(MORE_DATA);
    CALL ADD_TO_LIST;
    GET LIST(INPUT);
END;
CALL PRINT_LIST;
STOP;


ADD_TO_LIST: PROCEDURE;
ALLOCATE NODE; NODE.NAME = INPUT;
                 NODE.LINK = NULL;
IF HEAD = NULL
THEN HEAD = P;
/* becomes the first and only element of the list */
ELSE DO;
    LAST, CURRENT = HEAD;
    INSERTED = NO;
    DO WHILE( (CURRENT ^ = NULL) & (^ INSERTED));
        IF CURRENT -> NAME < P.NAME
        THEN DO;
            LAST = CURRENT;
            CURRENT = CURRENT -> LINK;
        END;
        ELSE DO;
            P -> NODE.LINK = CURRENT;
            /* or P -> LINK = CURRENT */
            LAST -> NODE.LINK = P;
            /* or LAST -> LINK = P */
            INSERTED = YES;
        END;
    END;
END;
IF ^ INSERTED THEN LAST -> NODE.LINK = P;
/* goes at end of the list */
```

```
END ADD_TO_LIST;

PRINT-LIST: PROCEDURE;
CURRENT = HEAD;
DO WHILE(CURRENT ^= NULL);
    PUT SKIP LIST(CURRENT -> NAME);
    CURRENT = CURRENT-> LINK;
END;
```

Figure 6

CHAPTER 10

FILE PROCESSING

10.1 BASIC CONCEPTS

Records in a file may be accessed either sequentially or directly. The *sequential access technique* is used to read all records in a file. The *direct access technique* is used to access a record directly by means of a *key*. In PL/1, there are two kinds of keys: recorded keys and source keys. A *recorded key* is a character string that immediately precedes each record in the data set to identify that record. The recorded key may be from 1 to 255 characters long. This length is either specified through *job control statements* or through the KEYLENGTH option of the ENVIRONMENT attribute in the file declaration statement. A *source key* is the character string value specified in the record-oriented I/O statements following the KEY or KEYFROM options.

The physical placement of records in a data set is guided by the chosen *file organization*. PL/1 supports four file organizations: CONSECUTIVE; INDEXED; REGIONAL; and VSAM, the first three of which are briefly examined in the following sections.

10.2 *CONSECUTIVE* FILE ORGANIZATION

In CONSECUTIVE file organization, a new record is simply added to the end of the file. The records are in no particular order except the order in which they were added to the file. Records may not be inserted in the middle of the file except by creating a new version of the file. A desired record can only be located by a sequential scan of the records in the file starting with the first record in the file.

CONSECUTIVE organization is the only file organization that can be used with sequential access storage devices (i.e., magnetic tapes), in which case, updating a record also requires rewriting the entire file and creating a new version. If the CONSECUTIVE file is stored on direct access storage devices (DASD), i.e., disks, updating a record *in place* becomes possible. This is specified by the UPDATE attribute in the file declaration statement.

```
// JOB M-D25597 020 002
                165484561,MBR0664,M -D,000,DADASH
FILEDEF CSCFILE DISK PRGRM7 OUT A1
                (RECFM F LRECL 20 BLOCK 20)
PLICG *
/* This program creates and lists a CONSECUTIVE disk file. */
PRGRM7: PROCEDURE OPTIONS(MAIN);
/* WORK_RECORD is the input/output record for the file. */
DECLARE 1 WORK_RECORD,
                2 NAME CHARACTER(15),
                2 NUMBER PICTURE '99999';
/* CSCFILE is the file to be created. */
DECLARE CSCFILE SEQUENTIAL RECORD
                ENVIRONMENT(CONSECUTIVE F
                RECSIZE(20) BLKSIZE(20));
DECLARE (EOF_CARDS, EOF_FILE) BIT(1) INITIAL('0'B);
```

84

```
ON ENDFILE(SYSIN) EOF_CARDS = '1'B;

OPEN FILE(CSCFILE) OUTPUT;
GET EDIT(WORK_RECORD) (COLUMN(1), A(15), A(5));
DO WHILE(^ EOF_CARDS);
    WRITE FILE(CSCFILE) FROM (WORK_RECORD);
    GET EDIT(WORK_RECORD) (COLUMN(1), A(15), A(5));
END;
CLOSE FILE(CSCFILE);

OPEN FILE(CSCFILE) INPUT;
ON ENDFILE(CSCFILE) EOF_FILE = '1'B;

READ FILE(CSCFILE) INTO(WORK_RECORD);
DO WHILE(^ EOF FILE);
    NUMBER = 2 * NUMBER;
    PUT SKIP EDIT(NAME, NUMBER) (A(15), X(3), A(5));
    READ FILE(CSCFILE) INTO(WORK_RECORD);
END;
CLOSE FILE(CSCFILE);

END PRGRM7;
/*
FIFTEEN LETTERS 789
ABC        12345
*/
/&
```

Figure 7

Figure 7 presents a *job deck* for compiling and executing a
PL/1 program in batch mode under the IBM VM operating
system. The program reads data cards containing a name and a
number and writes them to a CONSECUTIVE disk file. The
file is then processed sequentially and for each record, the
name and twice the number stored in the record are printed out.

10.3 *INDEXED* FILE ORGANIZATION

In INDEXED file organization, the records are stored in *source key sequence*. This means that a sequential scan of the file will produce the records in source key order. Furthermore, since an index is maintained, it is possible to directly access a record by specifying its source key value. As such, the PL/1 INDEXED file processing is commonly referred to as Indexed Sequential Access Method (ISAM).

The essential principles are illustrated by the program in Figure 8. The program reads data cards containing a name and a number and *adds* them to an existing INDEXED file which uses the name value as the source key. (The only allowable access method for *creation* of an INDEXED file is sequential; later, records can be added in direct access mode.) The file is then processed sequentially and for each record, the name and twice the number stored in the record are printed out. The resulting output will be in alphabetical order of the names. The following annotations refer to the line numbers in Figure 8, which are not part of the actual program.

Lines 2-4. Declaration of the record format for the ISAM file.

Line 5. Declaration of the program variable ISAMFILE as a record-oriented, keyed file with the following environment attributes: indexed; fixed-length record format; record size of 20 bytes; unblocked (block size is the same as record size); and a key length of 15 bytes.

Line 8. The ISAM file is opened for update in direct access mode.

Lines 9-12. A necessary on-unit when dealing with keyed

files. The KEY condition can be raised during the execution of the program if there is an attempt to add a duplicate record (i.e., having the same value for the name source key as another record) during a WRITE operation. The on-unit specifies that in such a case the duplicate name be printed out and the processing continue.

```
1.   PRGRM8: PROCEDURE OPTIONS(MAIN);
2.   DECLARE 1 WORK_RECORD,
3.        2 NAME CHARACTER(15),
4.        2 NUMBER PICTURE '99999';
5.   DECLARE ISAMFILE RECORD KEYED ENV(INDEXED F
             RECSIZE(20) BLKSIZE(20) KEYLENGTH(15));
6.   DECLARE (EOF_CARDS, EOF_FILE) BIT(1) INITIAL('O'B);

7.   ON ENDFILE(SYSIN) EOF_CARDS = '1'B;

8.   OPEN FILE(ISAMFILE) DIRECT UPDATE;
9.   ON KEY(ISAMFILE)
10.  BEGIN;
11.      PUT SKIP(2) EDIT('Duplicate: ', NAME) (A(20), A);
12.  END;

13.  GET EDIT(WORK_RECORD) (COLUMN(1), A(15), A(5));
14.  DO WHILE(^ EOF_CARDS);
15.      WRITE FILE(ISAMFILE) FROM (WORK_RECORD)
             KEYFROM(WORK RECORD.NAME);
16.      GET EDIT(WORK_RECORD) (COLUMN(1), A(15), A(5));
17.  END;
18.  CLOSE FILE(ISAMFILE);

19.  OPEN FILE(ISAMFILE) SEQUENTIAL INPUT;
20.  ON ENDFILE(ISAMFILE) EOF_FILE = '1'B;
```

```
21.   READ FILE(ISAMFILE) INTO(WORK_RECORD);
22.   DO WHILE(^ EOF_FILE);
23.       NUMBER = 2 * NUMBER;
24.       PUT SKIP EDIT(NAME, NUMBER) (A(15), X(3), A(5));
25.       READ FILE(ISAMFILE) INTO(WORK_RECORD);
26.   END;
27.   CLOSE FILE(ISAMFILE);

28.   END PRGRM8;
```

Figure 8

Line 13. The GET EDIT statement reads data from the card directly into the structure variable WORK_RECORD.

Line 15. The WRITE statement is used to write the record into the ISAM file. The KEYFROM options specifies the source key value for the record which will be used to determine the proper place to insert the record in the data set as well as to create an index entry in the associated index for the file.

Line 19. The ISAM file is opened for sequential processing.

Lines 20-27. Sequential processing of an ISAM file is identical to processing a CONSECUTIVE file. An on-unit for the ENDFILE condition is specified and the records are retrieved by the READ statement. Unlike CONSECUTIVE organization, however, the records produced by successive READ statements will be in (source key) order.

To maintain a file when records need to be modified or deleted, PL/1 provides the REWRITE and the DELETE statements. The REWRITE statement is used to update an *existing* record. (A WRITE statement is used when creating a file or adding a new record to an existing file.) The DELETE statement is used to remove a record from the file.

10.4 *REGIONAL* FILE ORGANIZATION

The PL/1 programmer may fully exploit the flexibility of direct access storage devices through the REGIONAL file organization. At the most abstract level, REGIONAL files appear and act like arrays. The REGIONAL file is divided into a collection of *regions* numbered consecutively from zero. REGIONAL(1) and REGIONAL(2) organizations allow only one record per region. By contrast, REGIONAL(3) organization allows more than one record to be stored in each region. In either of the three variations, it is the programmer's responsibility to specify in which region a new record is to be stored.

When a REGIONAL file is first created (i.e., it is OPENed for OUTPUT in DIRECT access mode), it will be automatically filled with *dummy records*. In the course of sequential processing of a REGIONAL(2) or REGIONAL(3) file, these dummy records will be automatically ignored by the READ statement. This can be done, because in REGIONAL(2) and REGIONAL(3) organizations each stored record is identified by a *recorded key* preceding the stored record; and, for dummy records, the first byte of the recorded key is filled with (8)'1'B. This is not the case with REGIONAL(1) files and the programmer must distinguish the dummy records from legitimate ones (which is usually accomplished by reserving the first byte of the logical record declaration as a flag character).

To add a record to a REGIONAL(1) file, the desired region number need only be specified. For example, the statement WRITE(REG1 FILE) FROM(REG_REC) KEYFROM('2131'); would identify the record as belonging in region 2131 (that is, the 2132nd record in the data set). To add a record to a RE-

89

GIONAL(2) file, declared by the statement DECLARE REG2FILE RECORD KEYED ENVIRONMENT(RE-GIONAL(2) F RECSIZE(100) KEYLENGTH(3));, both the desired region number and the desired recorded key must be specified. For example, WRITE(REG2FILE) FROM(REG_ REC) KEYFROM('543' I I '00002131');, which would cause the record to be written to region 2131 with an attached recorded key of '543'.

Figure 9 presents a *job deck* for compiling and executing a PL/1 program in batch mode under the IBM VM operating system. The program reads ten data cards each of which contains an employee name and an employee number (ranging from 01 to 10). The information is written to a REGIONAL(1) disk file with the employee number value (ranging from 01 to 10) determining the region number. The file is then processed sequentially and the names are printed out in region number (i.e., in this case, in employee number) order.

```
// JOB M-D25597 020 002
                165484561,MBR0664,M-D,000,DADASH
FILEDEF REGFILE DISK PRGRM9 OUT A1
                (RECFM F LRECL 19 BLOCK 19 XTENT 11)
PLICG *
/* This program creates and lists a REGIONAL(1) disk file. */
PRGRM9: PROCEDURE OPTIONS(MAIN);
/* WORK_RECORD is the input/output record for the file. */
DECLARE 1 WORK_RECORD,
                2 EMPLOYEE_NAME PICTURE '(17)X',
                2 EMPLOYEE_NUMBER PICTURE 'XX';
/* REGFILE is the file to be created. */
DECLARE REGFILE RECORD DIRECT KEYED
                ENVIRONMENT(REGIONAL(1)  F  RECSIZE(19));
DECLARE EOF_CARDS BIT(1) INITIAL('0'B);

ON ENDFILE(SYSIN) EOF_CARDS = '1'B;
```

90

```
/* Note that the file need not be initialized to "dummy records". */
OPEN FILE(REGFILE) UPDATE;
GET EDIT(WORK_RECORD) (COLUMN(1), A(17), X(3), A(2));
DO WHILE(^ EOF_CARDS);
    REWRITE FILE(REGFILE) FROM(WORK_RECORD)
            KEY(EMPLOYEE_NUMBER);
    GET EDIT(WORK_RECORD) (COLUMN(1),
            A(17), X(3), A(5));
END;
CLOSE FILE(REGFILE);

OPEN FILE(REGFILE) INPUT;
DO I = 1 TO 10;
    READ FILE(REGFILE) INTO(WORK_RECORD) KEY(I);
    PUT SKIP EDIT(EMPLOYEE_NUMBER,
            EMPLOYEE_NAME) (A(3), A(17));
END;
CLOSE FILE(REGFILE);

END PRGRM9;
/*
HUGHES, JOAN K.        04
CONWAY, RICHARD        01
GRIES, DAVID           03
KATZAN, HARRY          05
PRATT, TERRENCE        07
DAVIDSON, MELVIN       02
POLLACK, SEYMOUR       06
STERLING, THEODOR      09
ROCKEY, CLARENCE       08
TUCKER, ALLEN          10
*/
/&
```

Figure 9

91

CHAPTER 11

ADDITIONAL FEATURES

11.1 ABBREVIATIONS AND SHORTCUTS

Many of the PL/1 keywords can be abbreviated. Some common abbreviations are: BIN (BINARY), CHAR (CHARACTER), COL (COLUMN), COND (CONDITION), CONV (CONVERSION), DEC (DECIMAL), DCL (DECLARE), DEF (DEFINED), ENV (ENVIRONMENT), GOTO (GO TO), INIT (INITIAL), PIC (PICTURE), PTR (POINTER), PROC (PROCEDURE), SEQUENTIAL (SEQL), and VAR (VARYING).

A common shortcut in typing PL/1 programs is to use *factored attributes*. This refers to declaring a group of variables that have identical attributes using a single DECLARE statement. The general form of a factored DECLARE statement is: DECLARE (var1, var2, ...) common_attributes;, where some variables may be arrays with their dimensions, or DECLARE (array1, array2, ...) (common_dimensions) common_attributes;, where the arrays all have the same dimensions. The names of the variables are separated by commas, and the list is enclosed in parentheses. For example: DCL (FLAG_1, FLAG_2, FALSE) BIT(1) INIT('0'B);.

Two other common shortcuts in PL/1 are the use of *repetition factors* and *iteration factors*. A repetition factor is a number enclosed in parentheses that immediately precedes a character string, e.g., (5)'– ='. It instructs the compiler to generate a character string composed of the specified number of repetitions of the specified string, i.e., '– = – = – = – = – =' in this case. An iteration factor is a number enclosed in parentheses that immediately precedes non-character string data, e.g., (5) 0. It instructs the compiler to generate as many units of the value as specified by the iteration factor, i.e., five zeros in this case. Iteration factors are commonly used when initializing arrays. For example, DCL A(12) FIXED BIN INIT((12) 0);.

Another permissible shortcut is to use one DECLARE statement to declare several variables by separating each set of variables and their attributes by commas:

```
DCL    var1 attributes,
       (var2, var3) common_attributes,
       array1(dimensions) attributes,
       1 major_structure1, 2 elementary_item1, . . .,
       . . . ,
       varN attributes;
```

Although permissible, this shortcut should be avoided since it hampers program readability, especially if each variable does not appear on a separate line.

11.2 DEBUGGING AIDS

The time-honored way to find bugs in a program is the trace method. There are two types of trace. Value trace is a trace of the values of variables at various points in the program. Control flow trace is a trace of the flow of execution as GO TO statements, CALL statements, and function references are performed. PL/1, and especially the PL/C compiler, provide excellent support for both types of trace.

The PL/1 optimizing compiler provides a number of debugging facilities including an alphabetized cross-reference listing of variables, labels, and entry names. It also has an option for producing a graphical indication of the program's structure: the nesting of internal procedures, BEGIN blocks, and DO groups.

One of the most convenient tools for debugging is the PUT DATA statement, since it is easy to insert in a program and will cause both the name of a variable and its value to be printed out. In fact, the PUT DATA; statement without a data list, will cause *all* variables known to the program at the point of the PUT statement to be output.

PL/1's main vehicle for tracing values as well as controlling flow is the CHECK condition. To display the value of a variable, say 1, whenever it is assigned a new value by an input or an assignment statement, we can append a (CHECK(I)): prefix to the program. If we want a statement label, say L, to be displayed each time that statement is executed, we can append a (CHECK(L)): prefix to the program.

A dynamic aid for debugging is a programmer-defined ON condition. A defined condition can only be raised with the SIGNAL statement and is always enabled. Thus instead of inserting debugging statements in several places in the program, the programmer can establish a sequence of debugging statements by:

```
ON CONDITION(DEBUG)
    BEGIN;
        debugging statements;
    END;
```

and subsequently activate them from anywhere in the program with a SIGNAL(DEBUG); statement. After the DEBUG on-unit is executed, control returns to the statement following the SIGNAL statement.

There are several normally disabled conditions that should be enabled for program debugging purposes. They include the SUBSCRIPTRANGE condition which is raised whenever there is a reference to an element outside the bounds of an array; the STRINGRANGE condition which is raised whenever the arguments of the SUBSTR built-in function reference a nonexistent part of string data; and the STRINGSIZE condition which is raised when a string is about to be assigned to a shorter string.

One of the most useful on-units for debugging purposes is the ERROR on-unit. For all of the conditions that can raise during the execution of a program, a *standard system action* exists as part of PL/1. In the absence of programmer specified on-units, a standard system action will take place. For most conditions, the standard system action is to print a message and then raise the ERROR condition. The standard system action for the ERROR condition is to terminate the program and return control to the operating system. Therefore, whenever the ERROR condition is raised, the program is about to be terminated. By specifying the following on-unit for the ERROR condition we can obtain useful information for debugging purposes:

```
ON ERROR
    BEGIN;
        ON ERROR SYSTEM; /* take the system action if ERROR
        is raised during this block */
        PUT DATA;
    END;
```

Finally, PL/1 provides several built-in functions that are useful in handling on-units for specific conditions. The ONCODE function returns the code for the type of interrupt that caused entry into the active on-unit. For example, in an on-unit for the KEY condition, the ONCODE function can be used to determine if the cause of error was a duplicate key value or that the specified key value was not found. The appropriate codes may be found in the reference manual for the PL/1 compiler you are using.

The ONCHAR and the ONSOURCE built-in functions are used in an on-unit for the CONVERSION condition which is raised when there is an attempt to convert a character string to an arithmetic value where the character string contains characters other than numbers. The ONCHAR function extracts the character that caused the CONVERSION condition to be raised. The ONSOURCE function extracts the contents of the field that was being processed when the CONVERSION condition was raised. A useful generic on-unit for the CONVERSION condition is as follows:

```
ON CONVERSION
    BEGIN;
        PUT SKIP LIST('Conversion error in procedure '
                        | | ONLOC);
        PUT SKIP LIST('ONCODE = ' | | ONCODE);
        PUT SKIP LIST('Source field causing error '''
                        | | ONSOURCE | | '''.');
        PUT SKIP LIST('Source field changed to zero to
                        continue processing.');
        (NOSTRINGSIZE): /* disable STRINGSIZE condition */
            ONSOURCE = (16)'0';
    END;
```

11.3 TERMINAL I/O

When executing a PL/1 program interactively, the terminal becomes both the standard input (SYSIN) and the standard output file (SYSPRINT). As such, normal stream I/O statements may be used. However, the programmer must determine the end of file condition, i.e., ENDFILE(SYSIN), somewhat differently, usually by using a *sentinel* value to signify the end of input data.

The DISPLAY statement of PL/1 is particularly suited for writing interactive programs. It has the general form: DISPLAY *(expression)* REPLY *(character variable)*. When this statement is executed, the *expression* is evaluated and when necessary converted to a string of at most 72 characters. This string is then displayed on the terminal. If the REPLY option is specified, the program is suspended until a line is typed from the terminal. This line is then padded on the right with blanks or truncated on the right to result in a string of 126 characters which is assigned to the *character variable* and execution continues.

The following program demonstrates the DISPLAY statement and offers several procedures to make interactive programming in PL/1 easier.

```
PRGRM10: PROCEDURE OPTIONS(MAIN);
DECLARE INPUT_BUFFER(2) CHAR(70) VARYING;
DECLARE (INTNUM1, INTNUM2, ANSWER) FIXED
                DECIMAL(6,0);
DECLARE STRTOINT ENTRY RETURNS(DECIMAL FIXED(6,0)),
                STRTOREAL ENTRY RETURNS(FLOAT);
DECLARE TRUE BIT(1) INIT('1'B),
        FALSE BIT(1) INIT('0'B);
DECLARE ONSOURCE BUILTIN;
```

97

```
DISPLAY('Your name, please. (anywhere on the line)')
                        REPLY(INPUT_BUFFER(1));
CALL NUGGET(INPUT_BUFFER(1));
/* strip off leading and trailing blanks */

DISPLAY('Enter first number.') REPLY(INPUT_BUFFER(2));
CALL NUGGET(INPUT_BUFFER(2));

INTNUM1 = STRTOINT(INPUT_BUFFER(2));
/* convert number from character to integer */

DISPLAY('Enter second number.') REPLY(INPUT_BUFFER(2));
CALL NUGGET(INPUT_BUFFER(2));
 INTNUM2 = STRTOINT(INPUT_BUFFER(2));

ANSWER = INTNUM1 + INTNUM2; /* add the two numbers */
/* put the answer back into character representation. */
/* let PL/1 handle this conversion, since no error can occur. */
INPUT_BUFFER(2) = ANSWER;

DISPLAY('Your name:'); DISPLAY(INPUT_BUFFER(1));
DISPLAY('Sum of the two numbers: ', INPUT_BUFFER(2));
STOP;

STRTOINT: PROCEDURE(STR) RETURNS(DECIMAL FIXED(6,0));
/* returns integer value of string argument */
    DECLARE STR CHAR(70) VARYING;
    DECLARE INT DECIMAL FIXED (6,0);
    DECLARE TEMP CHAR (15) VARYING;
    ON CONVERSION ONSOURCE = '0'; TEMP = STR;
                    INT = TEMP;
    RETURN (INT);
END STRTOINT;
```

```
STRTOREAL: PROCEDURE(STR) RETURNS(FLOAT);
/* NOT REFERENCED IN EXAMPLE */
/* returns real value of string argument */
    DECLARE STR CHAR(70) VARYING;
    DECLARE REAL DECIMAL FIXED (6,0);
    DECLARE TEMP CHAR (15) VARYING;
    ON CONVERSION ONSOURCE = '0'; TEMP = STR;
                        INT = TEMP;
    RETURN (REAL);
END STRTOREAL;

NUGGET: PROCEDURE(STR);
/* strips off leading and trailing blanks */
DECLARE STR CHAR(70) VARYING;

    STRIP_FRONT: PROCEDURE;
    DECLARE (I, LEN) DECIMAL FIXED;
    DECLARE C CHAR(1);
    DECLARE NULL CHAR(1) INIT('0');
    LEN = LENGTH (STR); I = 1; C = SUBSTR(STR, I, 1);
    DO WHILE ( (I <= LEN) & (C = ' ' | C = NULL) );
        I = I + 1; C = SUBSTR(STR, I, 1);
    END;
    STR = SUBSTR(STR, I, LEN-I+1);
    END STRIP_FRONT;

    STRIP_REAR: PROCEDURE;
    DECLARE (I, LEN) DECIMAL FIXED;
    DECLARE C CHAR(1);
    DECLARE NULL CHAR(1) INIT('0');
    LEN = LENGTH (STR); I = LEN; C = SUBSTR(STR, I, 1);
    DO WHILE ( (I > 1) & (C = ' ' | C = NULL) );
        I = I - 1; C = SUBSTR(STR, 1, I);
    END;
```

```
      STR = SUBSTR(STR, 1, I);
      END STRIP_REAR;

/* call the two routines that do the work */
CALL STRIP_FRONT;
CALL STRIP_REAR;
END NUGGET;

END PRGRM10;
```

HANDBOOK OF
MATHEMATICAL,
SCIENTIFIC, and
ENGINEERING
FORMULAS, TABLES, FUNCTIONS, GRAPHS, TRANSFORMS

A particularly useful reference for those in math, science, engineering and other technical fields. Includes the most-often used formulas, tables, transforms, functions, and graphs which are needed as tools in solving problems. The entire field of special functions is also covered. A large amount of scientific data which is often of interest to scientists and engineers has been included.

Available at your local bookstore or order directly from us by sending in coupon below.

THE PROBLEM SOLVERS

The "PROBLEM SOLVERS" are comprehensive supplemental textbooks de signed to save time in finding solutions to problems. Each "PROBLEM SOLVER" is the firs of its kind ever produced in its field. It is the product of a massive effort to illustrate almos any imaginable problem in exceptional depth, detail, and clarity. Each problem is worke out in detail with step-by-step solution, and the problems are arranged in order of complexit from elementary to advanced. Each book is fully indexed for locating problems rapidly.

ADVANCED CALCULUS
ALGEBRA & TRIGONOMETRY
AUTOMATIC CONTROL
   SYSTEMS/ROBOTICS
BIOLOGY
BUSINESS, MANAGEMENT,
   & FINANCE
CALCULUS
CHEMISTRY
COMPLEX VARIABLES
COMPUTER SCIENCE
DIFFERENTIAL EQUATIONS
ECONOMICS
ELECTRICAL MACHINES
ELECTRIC CIRCUITS
ELECTROMAGNETICS
ELECTRONIC COMMUNICATIONS
ELECTRONICS
FINITE & DISCRETE MATH
FLUID MECHANICS/DYNAMICS
GENETICS

GEOMETRY:
PLANE • SOLID • ANALYTIC
HEAT TRANSFER
LINEAR ALGEBRA
MACHINE DESIGN
MECHANICS : STATICS • DYNAMICS
NUMERICAL ANALYSIS
OPERATIONS RESEARCH
OPTICS
ORGANIC CHEMISTRY
PHYSICAL CHEMISTRY
PHYSICS
PRE-CALCULUS
PSYCHOLOGY
STATISTICS
STRENGTH OF MATERIALS &
   MECHANICS OF SOLIDS
TECHNICAL DESIGN GRAPHICS
THERMODYNAMICS
TRANSPORT PHENOMENA :
MOMENTUM • ENERGY • MASS
VECTOR ANALYSIS

If you would like more information about any of these books, complete the coupo below and return it to us or go to your local bookstore.

RESEARCH and EDUCATION ASSOCIATION
61 Ethel Road W. • Piscataway • New Jersey 08854
Phone: (201) 819-8880

Please send me more information about your Problem Solver Books

Name _____

Address _____

City _____ State _____ Zip _____

HANDBOOK AND GUIDE FOR
COMPARING and SELECTING
COMPUTER LANGUAGES

BASIC	PL/1
FORTRAN	APL
PASCAL	ALGOL-60
COBOL	C

- This book is the first of its kind ever produced in computer science.

- It examines and highlights the differences and similarities among the eight most widely used computer languages.

- A practical guide for selecting the most appropriate programming language for any given task.

- Sample programs in all eight languages are written and compared side-by-side. Their merits are analyzed and evaluated.

- Comprehensive glossary of computer terms.

Available at your local bookstore or order directly from us by sending in coupon below.

RESEARCH and EDUCATION ASSOCIATION
61 Ethel Road W., Piscataway, New Jersey 08854
Phone: (201) 819-8880

VISA · MasterCard

Charge Card Number

Please check one box:
- ☐ Payment enclosed
- ☐ Visa
- ☐ Master Card

Expiration Date _____ / _____
                Mo   Yr

Please ship the "Computer Languages Handbook" @ $8.95 plus $2.00 for shipping.

Name _____

Address _____

City _____ State _____ Zip _____